ST. THOMAS AND
FORM AS
SOMETHING DIVINE
IN THINGS

THE AQUINAS LECTURE, 2007

ST. THOMAS AND FORM AS SOMETHING DIVINE IN THINGS

LAWRENCE DEWAN, O.P.

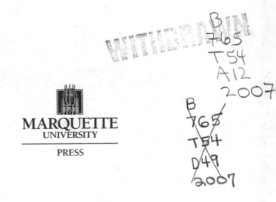

MARQUETTE
UNIVERSITY
PRESS

Under the auspices of the
Wisconsin-Alpha Chapter of Phi Sigma Tau

Library of Congress Cataloging-in-Publication Data

Dewan, Lawrence, 1932-
  St. Thomas and form as something divine in things
/ by Lawrence Dewan.
     p. cm. — (The Aquinas lecture ; 2007)
  Includes bibliographical references.
  ISBN 978-0-87462-174-7 (hardcover : alk. paper)
  1. Thomas, Aquinas, Saint, 1225?-1274. 2. Form
(Philosophy) 3. Aristotle. 4. Plato. I. Title. II.
Title: Saint Thomas and form as something divine in
things.
B765.T54D47 2007
117—dc22
                                              2006039580

Printed in the United States of America.

♾The paper used in this publication meets the minimum requirements of the
American National Standard for Information Sciences—
Permanence of Paper for Printed Library Materials, ANSI Z39.48-1992.

MARQUETTE UNIVERSITY PRESS
MILWAUKEE

The Association of Jesuit University Presses

PREFATORY

The Wisconsin-Alpha Chapter of Phi Sigma Tau, the International Honor Society for Philosophy at Marquette University, each year invites a scholar to deliver a lecture in honor of St. Thomas Aquinas.

The 2007 Aquinas Lecture, *St. Thomas and Form as Something Divine in Things*, was delivered on Sunday, February 25, 2007, by the Reverend Lawrence Dewan, O.P., Professor of Philosophy at Dominican University College, Ottawa, and Adjunct Professor of Philosophy, University of Ottawa.

Lawrence Dewan was born in North Bay, Ontario, Canada, studied philosophy at St. Michael's College of the University of Toronto, and received his Ph.D. in Philosophy from the University of Toronto in 1967. His Ph.D. Dissertation, begun under Étienne Gilson and completed under Rev. Joseph Owens, C.Ss.R., is entitled "The Doctrine of Being of John Capreolus: A Contribution to the History of the Notion of *Esse*." After teaching in several universities, he joined the Dominican Order in 1973, received an M.A. in Theology from the Dominican University College, and was ordained in 1976.

Since 1974 Fr. Dewan has been a member of the faculty of Dominican University College, where he also served as Vice-President from 1984-1990. He has been Visiting Professor of Philosophy in the Pontifical Institute of Mediaeval Studies and the University of Toronto, from 1983-1989; in the School of Philosophy of the Catholic University of America, Washington, D.C., from 1990-1997; and in 2005 at the International Theological Institute, Gaming, Austria. In 2003 he was Lokuang Chair in Philosophy at the Institute of Scholastic Philosophy, Fu Jen Catholic University, Taipei, Republic of China.

Among other honors, Fr. Dewan has been President of the Canadian Jacques Maritain Association from 1988-1995, and President of the American Catholic Philosophical Association, 1992-1993. In 1998 he was named Master of Sacred Theology by the Dominican Order. He was elected a member of the Pontifical Academy of St. Thomas Aquinas in 1999.

In addition to his volume, *Form and Being: Studies in Thomistic Metaphysics*, and a forthcoming companion volume in ethics, Fr. Dewan has published over a hundred papers in the history of philosophy, metaphysics, natural theology, epistemology, and ethics. Among the titles are: "St. Thomas, Metaphysics, and Formal Causality," "St. Thomas, Joseph Owens, and Existence,"

"The Individual as a Mode of Being According to Thomas Aquinas," "OBIECTUM: Notes on the Invention of a Word," "St. Thomas and Pre-Conceptual Knowledge," "St. Albert, the Sensibles, and Spiritual Being," "Distinctiveness of St. Thomas' Third Way," "St. Thomas and the Divine Names."

To Fr. Dewan's distinguished list of publications, Phi Sigma Tau is pleased to add: *St. Thomas and Form as Something Divine in Things*.

ST. THOMAS AND FORM AS SOMETHING DIVINE IN THINGS

LAWRENCE DEWAN, O.P.

THE APPROPRIATENESS OF CONSIDERING SUBSTANTIAL FORM

In recent years there has been much public discussion of biological evolution, and in particular of the Neo-Darwinian conception of evolution, as contrasted with Design Theory. The issue, I would say, is what sort of being and what sort of origin form has. The discussion of form as such pertains to metaphysics,[1] and so I thought that we might benefit from a reflection on form.

The term "form" covers a field including much diversity, and in fact is one of those words said analogically, or according to priority and posteriority. By priority it is said of natural, substantial form, as contrasted to merely artificial or accidental form;

and primarily it is said of God: God is by his own essence form.[2] But we will come to that later.

The association of the topics of evolution and substantial form was very much on the mind of Étienne Gilson towards the end of his long career. In 1971 he published a book on final causality and what he called "biophilosophy,"[3] and in it he argued that substantial form is the necessary foundation for natural teleology.[4] Jacques Maritain, writing to congratulate him on the book, questioned Gilson's view that like the doctrine that each species is the object of a special divine creation, Darwin's own doctrine of the progressive formation of living things—a formation brought about of itself—was another "indemonstrable theology." Maritain asked:

> Don't you think…that the philosopher can legiti-
> mately hold as most probable the idea that the
> creative act was accomplished [by God] through
> time by evolution, whereas the coming on the
> scene of the human species was the object of a
> special creation in the case of the first human being
> (as, subsequently, for every human individual the
> creation of the spiritual soul)?[5]

Gilson's answer is what interests me today. We read:

> What separates us irreparably from [modern sci-
> ence] is the Aristotelian (and common sense)
> notion of Substantial Form…. Descartes rid nature

of it. They understand nothing anymore since they forgot Aristotle's great saying that "there is no part of an animal that is purely material or purely immaterial." It is not the word "philosophy," it is the word "nature" that separates us from our contemporaries. Since I do not have any hope of convincing them of the truth (which yet is evident) of hylomorphism, I do not believe it is possible to propose our hypothesis to them as scientifically valid.[6]

Accordingly, I have taken my cue from Gilson, and turned my attention to substantial form.

ARISTOTLE'S *PHYSICS* I AND THOMAS'S COMMENT

That Aristotle thought it a topic worthy of consideration one sees in books 7 and 8 of his *Metaphysics*. As St. Thomas taught, these central books have as their subject particular substantial form.[7] So also, the doctrine is central to Aristotle's *De anima*. And I take my title and theme from his presentation in *Physics* book 1, on substantial form as one of the principles of natural things. We read:

> For admitting with them [the Platonists] that there is something divine, good, and desirable, we hold that there are two other principles, the one contrary to it, the other such as of its own nature to desire and yearn for it.[8]

Thomas Aquinas is not innovating, then, with his teaching that form is something divine in things. Aristotle was there before him. We read in Thomas's paraphrasing commentary:

> ...form is something divine and best, an object of appetite. It is divine, because *every form* is something of a participation by likeness of the divine act of being [*divini esse*], which [divine act of being] is pure act: for, each thing just to this extent is actually [*est in actu*], that is, inasmuch as it *has form*. It is something best, because act is the perfection of potency and its good; and consequently it follows that it is an object of appetite, because each thing has appetite for its own perfection.[9]

Here, then, the doctrine of form as divine is arrived at from its giving the act of being to matter.[10] Since *God's* act of being is pure act,[11] and the form of the generated thing gives being in act to the thing, therefore the form is a participation by way of likeness to God. (We might note that Gilson's linking of form and finality, that is, goodness, is borne out by the statement of the *Physics* just quoted.)

We must reflect on each step here. Obviously, to present form as something divine in things, one has to present the divine, namely, God, and one has to present God as *ipsum esse subsistens*, the very act of being subsisting, and one has to present form as principle of being, *principium essendi*. We will do our best in the time allotted.

Since our meditation here aims to be philosophical, we must be concerned with "the way up," that is, we must not start with God but rather with the things more readily knowable to us. We must first focus on hylomorphism.

Some Remarks on the Word "Form" and Its Use in the History of Metaphysics

Something must be said about the philosophical vocabulary. Of course, the first meaning of "form" one finds (from among fourteen!) in an English dictionary is "shape, arrangement of parts, visible aspect (esp. apart from colour), shape of body (*face and form*)." Eventually one comes to the meaning (in third place, with the note "philosophical"):

> …that which makes anything (*matter*) a determinate species (Scholastic), conditions of thing's existence by knowing which we can produce it (Baconian), formative principle holding together the elements of thing (Kantian).[12]

And we will be working in the realm of such "philosophical" meaning.

How does one get from the more obvious to the philosophical? I think of some remarks of St. Thomas in connection with the conception of an "image." For example:

...we do not say that one who imitates someone in whiteness is the image of that one, but rather one who imitates in *shape* [*figura*], which is the proximate and express sign of the species and nature: for we see that of diverse species among animals the shapes are diverse.[13]

While one might begin with the vocabulary employed by Plato for form, as, for example, the Greek "*idea*" and "*eidos*,"[14] it is sufficient for our purposes to note the words used by Aristotle in a prominent passage. We find the term "*morphē*" in a key preliminary determination in *Metaphysics* 7.3. Aristotle lists four meanings of "*ousia*," translated here [by Ross] as "substance," the last of which is the "substratum." He says:

Now the substratum [*to hupokeimenon*] is that of which everything else is predicated, while it is itself not predicated of anything else. And so we must first determine the nature of this: for that which underlies a thing primarily is thought to be in the truest sense its substance. And in one sense matter [*hē hulē*] is said to be of the nature of substratum, in another, shape [*hē morphē*], and in a third the compound of these. (By the matter I mean, for instance, the bronze, by the shape the pattern of its form [*tēn de morphēn ta skēma tēs ideas*], and by the compound of these the statue, the concrete whole [*to sunolon*]. Therefore, if the form [*to eidos*] is prior [*proteron*] to the matter and more real [*mallon on*], it will be prior also to the compound of both, and for the same reason.

> We have now outlined the nature of substance,
> showing that it is that which is not predicated of a
> stratum, but of which all else is predicated. But we
> must not merely state the matter thus; for this is
> not enough. The statement itself is obscure....[15]

Notice that the translator here, Sir David Ross, has
rendered "*morphē*" as "shape," and most telling is
the use of the *statue* as stand-in, in the order of
artifacts, for the natural substance. Notice also
that we already have other key terms for what is
meant by "form" (the English word "form" brings
out the metaphor of shape quite well). We have
other Greek words already needed to get at what
we mean, thus both "*idea*" and "*eidos.*" And the
entire discussion is about what deserves the name:
"*ousia,*" that is, "entity" or "[what is truly] being."[16]
It is remarkable, also, that in this sketch Aristotle
immediately presents the form as "*more a being
[mallon on]*" than the matter is.[17] Form and act,
as Thomas will say, have *more* of the *ratio essendi*,
the intelligible character of being, than matter and
potency have.[18]

Thomas follows the Aristotelian vocabulary,
in Latin of course, interpreting the wider term
"*ousia,*" which he receives translated as "*substan-
tia,*" as "*forma*" when that is meant. For example,
Thomas paraphrases Aristotle as follows:

> ...that is the cause of something in the role of
> *substance*, namely, in the role of *form*, which is the

cause of being [*causa essendi*], for *through the form*
each thing is in act [*est actu*]. But the soul is the
cause of being for living things, for through the
soul they live; and living itself [*ipsum uiuere*] is
their being [*esse*]. Therefore, the soul is the cause
of living things in the role of *form*.[19]

In Aristotle's Greek the cause of *einai* (Latin *esse*),
is *ousia* (Latin *substancia*). This substantiality or
entity is what Thomas calls "form."

As Thomas presents books 7 and 8 of the *Meta-physics*, their subject, as we noted, is particular
substantial form, something in natural substances
analogous to the shape of the statue. Aristotle
eventually presents it as the principle of being.[20] He
begins the study of being with substance as found
in sensible, generable and corruptible substances.
Thus, a crucial point is that the definable nature
or species of such things is not purely form, but is
a composite of matter and form, though the form
is primary in the definition.[21] The effect of this
doctrine is to present a type of form which requires
for its intelligibility its perfecting of a matter. This
could well lead to the idea that what is meant by
"form" is something one can find *only* in matter.
Just as we will say that matter cannot exist without
form, so someone might think it right to say that
form cannot exist save as perfecting matter.

While there are some texts of Thomas which
use the word "form" in such a limited way, this

is not generally the case. Rather, "form" names a perfection that can be found subsisting without matter. The very *word* "form" is viewed as signifying what is found *most truly* in things transcending the material world. Thus, just as in the *De ente et essentia* Thomas teaches that *essence* is found more truly in simple substances than in composites, and most truly in God,[22] so in the *Summa theologiae* it is God who is presented as "*per essentiam suam forma*," form by his very essence, and as *primo et per se forma*, primary in the order of form. And this is based on the association of form as such with efficient causality: "every agent *acts* in function of its form."[23]

A Beacon Text

If asked to choose a text giving a good first idea of form as here meant, I think of the discussion in the *Summa theologiae* as to whether death is natural for the human being. I do so, not only to move from the realm of artifacts to that of natural substances, but also to go beyond mere mathematical form. In the text I have in mind Thomas presents the universe in which corruption obviously occurs. The question is whether it is "natural." Individual agents seek to perpetuate their being, but universal agent[s] regulate this cosmic situation so that equilibrium is maintained. Thus, we read:

...we can speak of each corruptible thing in two ways: in one way, in function of *universal* nature; in another way, in function of the *particular* nature.

The particular nature is *the intrinsic active conserving power* of each thing. And [taking the thing] in that latter way, all corruption and defect is *against nature*, as is said [by Aristotle] in *De caelo*, book 2.[24]

But universal nature is the active power in some universal principle of nature, for example, in one of the celestial bodies, or in some superior substance, according to which [perspective] some people call God "nature bringing about nature" [*natura naturans*]. Now, this power intends the good and conservation of the universe, which requires the alternation of generation and corruption in things.[25] And in that perspective corruptions and defects are natural, *not according to the inclination of the form, which is the principle of being and perfection,* but according to the inclination of the matter, which is proportionately attributed to such a form in accordance with the distribution of the universal agent.[26]

And though *every form intends the perpetuation of being to the extent that this is possible,* nevertheless no form of a corruptible thing can achieve its perpetuity save the rational soul, by the fact that it is not completely subject to corporeal matter as other forms are; indeed, it has its own immaterial operation, as was established in the First Part.[27]

It is such a principle of perpetuity that we mean by "form."[28] This is seen both in the individual seeking self-preservation through nutrition, etc., and through the individual as the embodiment of a specific nature.[29]

The Perennial Difficulty as Shown by the Presocratics, and the Platonic Solution

Aristotle provides us with a history of the problem of the recognition of form on the part of the philosophers. This is clearly a case of the situation spoken of by Gilson in the preface to his book *Being and Some Philosophers*:

> The present book is not an attempt to show what comes first in reality, for all philosophers know it inasmuch as they are, not philosophers, but men. Our only problem will be to know how it is that what men so infallibly know *qua* men, they so often overlook *qua* philosophers.[30]

Certainly if, as St. Thomas says, everything that is known is known through its form,[31] form must be rather obvious, well known to all. Yet problems there have been.

The most striking problem one finds among the ancient Greek cosmologists is that of coming to be. Unanimously they taught that nothing comes to be or ceases to be.

We should begin with the grasp of things as
substances, where by "substance" one means the
subsisting thing, the thing which has its *own being*,
as contrasted with the merely *inherent* item.[32] We
can indicate what we mean by contrasting "this
dog," named "Fido," with his shape or color or size
or weight. Shape, color, size, and weight are real
features of Fido, and yet are not identical with him.
Each of them is somewhat variable, while Fido
remains the identical[33] Fido. And, most important,
each of these features has *being* only *in* Fido. Each
of them, from the viewpoint of being, is an *inherent*. They have being only through dependence on
the being of Fido. Fido, on the other hand, "has"
being, and, indeed, has "his own" being.[34]

It was as regards the "being" which is proper to
the subsisting thing as such that the ancient Greek
philosophers, the presocratics, said that *nothing
comes to be or ceases to be*.[35] And they said this
while dealing with the evident fact that Fido does
cease to be, is no more. To explain this, they *down-
graded* the *being* of Fido. This comes out clearly, for
example, in texts from Empedocles, ca. 480 B.C.,
who proposed four fundamental "roots;" earth,
water, air, and fire (Aristotle interprets Empedocles
as giving them the status of smallest particles).[36]
Empedocles says:

> ...there is no birth of any of mortal things, nor
> any end in baneful death, but only a mixing and

an exchange of the things that have been mixed [Fragment 8].[37]

And:

But men, when these have been mixed in the form of a man and come into the light, or in the form of a species of wild animals, or plants, or birds, they say that this has "come into being;" and when they separate, this men call sad fate. The terms that Right demands they do not use; but through custom I myself also apply these names [Fragment 9].[38]

This philosopher, as we see, is a "particle physicist,"[39] and such items as the human being or the dog or the tree are mere alterations in the configurations of the ingenerable and incorruptible particles, the true substances or beings. True being simply is; there is no such thing as "coming to be" or "ceasing to be."

This is a phenomenon in the history of philosophy which I would say merits the description: "forgetfulness of being." It is only inasmuch as one appreciates the *unity* of the things we call "dogs" and "cats" and "human beings" that one will be obliged to treat them as "beings" in the unqualified sense of that word, and that one will be obliged to do the intellectual work involved in understanding how unqualified coming to be and ceasing to be are possible.

We might also note that Aristotle points to Empedocles as the adversary holding that natural kinds result from random mutation: what happens to fit survives.[40]

If we turn to Socrates as he is presented by Plato,[41] one of the greatest passages in Western literature is surely the autobiographical account given by Socrates at a most critical moment in the *Phaedo*. It has already been established to the satisfaction of Socrates' two most able interlocutors that the soul can survive the body. The remaining difficulty is to show that the thus surviving soul is not in itself such as eventually destined to cease to be. This requires, says Socrates, an investigation of the causes of coming to be and ceasing to be, and of being. Socrates recalls his youthful enthusiasm for the study of nature, and his frequenting the schools of the physicists. He remembers the questions asked in their school:

> Do heat and cold, by a sort of fermentation, bring about the organization of animals, as some people say? Is it the blood, or air, or fire by which we think?[42]

Their method is criticized because the focus is on the juxtaposition of sensible things from which a being results, and on the forces which put them together. This leaves unconsidered the *unity proper to the result of the process*, which is precisely what he wanted explained. Their whole approach leaves one in ignorance of what constitutes the unity of units: what makes a thing the "one" which it is. What makes one thing one?[43] This is precisely what Thomas will mean by "form."[44] The Platonic solution is already a doctrine of form (*ousia*),[45] but one which itself leaves difficulties.

ARISTOTLE AND FORM

As regards his predecessors, one of Aristotle's main points was their failure to conceive of the causes properly. *None* of the causes was seen as adequately spoken of.[46] Concerning the formal cause in particular, we are told:

> The essence [*to … ti ēn einai*], that is, the substantial reality [*tēn ousian*], no one has expressed distinctly. It is hinted at chiefly by those who believe in the Forms….[47]

Especially regarding the physical philosophers, he says:

> …they err in not positing the substance [*tēn ousian*], that is, the essence [*to ti esti*], as the cause of anything….[48]

The Platonic shortcoming we can see in the account of the human being in the *Phaedo*. The human being is there assessed as a soul imprisoned in a body (an imprisonment stemming from and maintained by our own ontological error).[49] Con-

trast this with the general doctrine of soul which
one has in Aristotle's *De anima* 2. There the question of what makes the soul one with the body is
called ill-formed. As Thomas Aquinas explains
the text, by the very fact that we are dealing with
a matter/form composite, we are dealing with
something one.[50]

The pedagogy in the approach to soul in the *De
anima* should not be neglected. We move from the
artifact, for example, an axe, to what is a natural
part, that is, an eye, and then to the whole animal.
Aristotle carefully distinguishes between the level
of actuality which we generally call "being," and
the level we call "operation." In the case of the axe
we focus, not on cutting, which is the operation,
a second level actuality, but on the sharpness of
the axe-head, the feature that makes the piece of
metal "to BE an axe:" sharpness would be the soul
of the axe, if the axe were a natural, living thing.
If we then move beyond the realm of the artificial
to the natural, but merely to a single organ of a
living thing, an eye, then seeing is not what we
focus on, but rather *the ability to see*; that is, not the
operation, but the *ability* to perform the operation:
this is what makes the eye "*to BE an eye*." If the eye
were a complete thing, the ability to see would be
its soul. This then is the lesson. The principle of
the living thing *as a whole* is the soul. It is what
makes the whole thing *unqualifiedly* "one." It is the

principle of being. It is thus a cause in the mode of "form."[51]

This doctrine is at one with the carefully worked out conception of substantial form in material substances, presented by Aristotle in *Metaphysics* 7 and 8: the form we encounter there is not the entire essence of the thing, though it is the principle of the essence. The essence, signified by the definition, is a composite of form and matter, taken universally. In other words, the form, though a principle of intelligibility, is here necessarily understood as the perfection *of matter*. This pertains to the doctrine of the being that belongs to generable and corruptible things. It is here that Aristotle improves on Plato, the Plato of the *Timaeus*, as we shall see next, providing a doctrine of unqualified being as attributable to the particular kinds of things in the sensible realm.[52]

THE ARISTOTELIAN HYLOMORPHIC DOCTRINE AND ITS DIFFICULTY

Let us begin by sympathizing with the Presocratic philosophers. Hylomorphism, the doctrine of generable substance as composed of matter and form, is not easy. Aristotle in *Physics* 4 remarks that *both matter and form are difficult to know*, pertaining to *the highest study*.[53] We should not be surprised, then, that the common error of the Presocratic phi-

losophers was, as we said, the judgment that nothing comes to be or ceases to be. Even the Platonic
account of sensible reality, taking that account in
its most physical mode, as in the *Timaeus*, did not
solve that problem. If we take Plato's presentation
of, for example, fire, one of the traditional elements, we find that the tableau presents the Idea of
Fire, and the Receptacle, and the Phenomenal Fire,
three items with three different modes of being.
Plato warns against considering the phenomenon
a "this." It is a mere "such." What is primary in
being is the Idea (akin to a father), what comes
second is the Receptacle (akin to a mother). The
phenomenon itself, what we commonly call "fire,"
is in third place ontologically. This means that
Plato is still in the position of the presocratics in
this respect, namely, that the subject of all change
has ontological priority over the sensible thing.[54]
We can have no doctrine of true coming *to be* and
ceasing *to be*.

The Aristotelian doctrine of primary matter will
provide the solution to the problem of unqualified
coming to be and ceasing to be. Aristotle explains
in *Physics* 1.9 the inadequacy of the Platonic conception of matter as "mother," a conception which
includes not only the potency to form, but also
the privation.[55] This makes the Platonic material
substratum something already intrinsically actual;
thus, there can be no unqualified coming to be.

Aristotle bases his own doctrine on the primacy, in our experience, of the dog, the cat, the human being. It is these (unities) that are primary beings.[56] Concerning them we note three most remarkable features, that is, that they are born and die, that they maintain themselves by nourishment, and that they reproduce. These features are combined in, for example, the production of a new lion by parent lions. This involves the killing and eating of, for example, an antelope by the parent lions. The ceasing to be of the antelope coincides[57] with the coming to be of lion (in matter previously actualized as antelope).[58] This is *unqualified ceasing to be* and coming *to be*, because "being a lion" and "being an antelope" are instances of unqualified "being." It is this event which reveals the nature of the primary matter and the causal role of substantial form.

We begin with the doctrine of substantial unity, such that "you are you through and through."[59] We consider that any change involves something one and the same being otherwise now than it was before.[60] We consider that what was an antelope is now a lion. By the "primary matter" we mean *the something one and the same* in such a change. We see that the nature of the matter underlying unqualified coming to be and ceasing to be must, just in itself, not have actually any *substantial* determination, positive or negative. It is intrinsically neither this nor not this. It is potentially all generable and corruptible natures.[61]

Such a substratum cannot be found alone. It has perfect being only through some present substantial determinant. In itself it has only the imperfect being required for such a role.[62]

The difficulty in knowing matter is stressed.[63] It is known only by analogy. As Thomas says:

> [Aristotle] says that the nature which is first subjected to change, that is, the primary matter, cannot be known through itself, *since everything which is known is known through its form*; but primary matter is seen as the subject of every form. But it is known through analogy, that is, through proportion.... Therefore, that which so stands relative to natural substances themselves as the bronze to the statue and the wood to the bed, and any material and unformed item to the form, this we say is primary matter.

> This, therefore, is one principle of nature. It is not one in the way that a "this something" [*hoc aliquid*] [is one], that is, as some indicated individual [*aliquod individuum demonstratum*] [is one], such that it has form and unity in act; but it is called "a being" and "one" inasmuch as it is *in potency to form*....[64]

And in *De generatione et corruptione* Aristotle speaks of how difficult it is to conceive of unqualified coming to be, precisely because of the difficulty of conceiving of primary matter: that which is

potentially a substantial actuality.[65] Only when it
is realized that such matter *never does or can exist
separately* is there a satisfactory solution to what
Aristotle describes as the "wondrous difficulty."
Primary matter exists only as part of the composite
of form and matter.[66]

Thus, Aristotle is very far from treating his primary items of analysis as ones which are familiar to
all. As we saw, regarding the physical philosophers
he says:

> ...they err in not positing the substance [*tēn
> ousian*], that is, the essence [*to ti esti*], as the cause
> of anything....[67]

If we fail to understand the form as cause, we will
also not understand the true nature and role of
matter.

PERENNIAL PRESOCRATISM

It is my contention that there is such a thing as
"perennial presocratism." The presocratics, like
the poor, we have always with us. And they are
to be found among those who are very successful
scientists (as was the case with the ancient Greek
presocratics; thus, Thales was famous for his pre-
diction of the solar eclipse of 585 B.C.).[68] The
ancient scientists were also metaphysicians, making judgments about the being of things (such as:

"nothing comes to be or ceases to be"). Aristotle affirmed this metaphysical ambition of theirs so strongly that, at the very moment when he was presenting the primary philosophy as seeking the science of beings as beings, he made his point by noting the resemblance of his own project with that of the ancient cosmologists. *They* sought the causes of being as being.[69]

If we consider a present-day successful scientist, for example, Nobelist Stephen Weinberg, what he is talking about sounds like something in the line of Aristotle's material cause. He says:

> Indeed, elementary particles are not in themselves very interesting, not at any rate in the way that people are interesting. Aside from their momentum and spin, every electron in the universe is just like every other electron—if you have seen one electron, you have seen them all. But this very simplicity suggests that electrons, unlike people, are not made up of numbers of more fundamental constituents, but are themselves something close to the fundamental constituents of everything else. It is because elementary particles are so boring that they are interesting; their simplicity suggests that the study of elementary particles will bring us closer to a fundamental study of nature.[70]

The simplicity Weinberg is speaking of seems to be that of fundamental constituents in the *potential* sense, items that are somehow "ready to be anything." In themselves, they offer little distinctive character to the observing mind.[71] It is significant that Weinberg thinks what he should be after is "fundamental constituents." This suggests that he looks to some elementary *kind of thing* as what is fundamental. In other words, he has not the idea of primary matter in the Aristotelian sense, and so his ontology is really mechanistic, which is to say that he sees all forms as accidental.[72]

Plato in the *Sophist* spoke of a war "always going on" between the earth-born giants and the friends of the forms, as to what is it is to "*be*." My speaking of perennial presocratism merely repeats this Platonic contention that there is "always" such a war.[73] The evolutionary scientist is, in spirit, very often a "primary philosopher," that is, a metaphysician, even if somewhat unconsciously.

I do not mean to suggest that scientists have an exclusive hold on error in this area. There was, for example, in medieval times the very influential thought of the theologian and poet Solomon Ibn Gabirol (1021-1058 A.D.). To judge by the effort expended by St. Thomas to refute him,[74] he must have been exceedingly popular. Thomas sees him as returning to the position of the ancient naturalists, the presocratics, who held that all things are one being, when they said that the substance of all things is matter (meaning by "matter" not a mere potential being, but an actual kind of thing). The

Gabirol reasoning reduced all form to accidental
form, eliminating not only the principles of physics
but even the principles of metaphysics:

> The aforementioned position does away…even
> with the principles of first philosophy, taking away
> unity from singular things, and consequently the
> true entity and diversity of things.[75]

Indeed, we know that the two propositions in
Thomas's teaching which were subjects of contro-
versy in his own time, so that he became an indirect
target in the Parisian condemnations of 1277, were
the impossibility for God even miraculously to
create matter without form, and the necessity for
a substance to have only one substantial form.[76]
A little later, Duns Scotus still thought that God
could create matter without form.[77]

So strong is the tendency to attribute some actuality to matter just in itself that even so ardent a
disciple of Thomas as Gilson, who, as we said at
the outset, underlined the importance of hylomorphism, nevertheless expressed himself in formulas
which surely cannot be accepted. Thus, we read:

> Potency is incomplete actuality considered in its
> aptitude to achieve a more complete state of actu-
> ality. [78]

No, we must insist that primary matter is *pure*
potency,[79] and "actuality and potentiality exclude
each other."[80]

SUBSTANCE AND FORM

If matter is often conceived of as having its own actuality, the intrinsic difficulty of conceiving potency is not the only reason. It is also possible to fail to think through the requirements of substance, and so of form.[81] Here I think first of Aristotle's wisdom in pointing to the importance of the preposition "in" in order to approach the nature of the first level of actuality. And I see the meaning of this "in" best conceived when one works one's way through Thomas's presentation of the truth that the whole soul is ⟨in⟩ every part of the body. But let us begin with Aristotle.

It is in the *De anima* that Aristotle presents soul as on the first level of actuality, in contrast to operation as on the second level. As we mentioned earlier, the soul of the whole animal is analogous to the sharpness of the axe, not to the operation of cutting. These modes of being in act are presented in *Metaphysics* 9. Act is first presented in a general way as conceived through a series of comparisons, that is, by analogy.[82] As Thomas paraphrases:

> Thus, if we take the proportion of (1) the one who is building to (2) one who is able to build; and [the proportion] of (1) someone awake to (2) one who is sleeping; and [the proportion] of (1) one who is seeing to (2) one who has his eyes closed but has the power of sight; and of (1) that which is

separated out from the matter, that is, that which
is formed through the operation of art or nature,
and thus is distinguished from unformed matter
[to (2) the matter];…of any pair so differing, one
of the items [designated "1"] will be the act and
the other [designated "2"] will be the potency.
And in this way, proportionally, [beginning] from
particular examples, we can come to a knowledge
of what act is and [what] potency [is].[83]

However, these comparisons present act in a
general way. The distinction between first and
second act is made by contrasting comparisons
using the preposition "in" (associated with first act)
with those using the preposition "to" (associated
with second act). As the sharpness is *in* the axe,
so the power of sight is *in* the eye. As the cutting
is *to* the axe, so seeing is *to* the eye.

The use of "to" sets up a comparison such that
both related items "stand out:" the one which has
the role of subjected item is *already* a "something,"
that is, already in "first act;" the other adds to it.
The use of "in," on the other hand, describes a pair
where the subjected item *is the something that it is
by virtue of the other member*: sharpness makes
the axe an axe, the power of vision makes the eye
an eye.

Aristotle thus associates what we call "form"
with the "in" type comparison. What we mean
by "form" is what imbues, permeates, and thus

intrinsically characterizes that in which it is.[84] This
is the reason why St. Thomas says that the act of
being, *ipsum esse*, which he presents as most *formal*
of all, is "inmost" relative to that which has it.[85]

This interiority suggests that form is pre-emi-
nently an object of intellect. As Thomas explains
the Latin word "*intellectus:*"

> The word "intellect" suggests a *deeply penetrating*
> knowledge: the [Latin] word "*intelligere*" suggests
> "reading the interiors." And this is quite clear to
> anyone considering the difference between *intel-
> lect* and *sense*. For, sense-knowledge has to do
> with *exterior sensible* qualities; whereas intellective
> knowledge penetrates right to the *essence* of the
> thing: for the object of the intellect is *what the
> thing is*....[86]

I have personally found helpful, in order to
reflect on this object, Thomas's presentation of the
truth that the whole soul is in every part of the
body. Our imagination is most at home, it seems,
with a sort of one to one correspondence in the
realm of bodies, a mechanical correspondence. If
we are told that form "imbues" the matter, this
suggests the way water permeates a sponge, this
part of the water in this part of the sponge, and
that in that. On the one hand, we need to use our
imagination in order to understand, and on the
other we must transcend the imagination in order
to understand.[87]

Thomas, in *ST* 1.76, is speaking of the specifi-
cally human soul and its union with the human
body. His main point is that this soul, which he
has already presented as *subsisting* form,[88] is the
substantial form of the human body. Thus, the
eight articles making up the question provide one
of the best places to study substantial form, in
general, as the principle of being of a body.

The last article asks whether the soul is present
in the whole of the human body. The key to an
answer is substantial form:

> …the substantial form is not merely the perfection
> of the whole, but of every part whatsoever. For
> since the whole is constituted out of the parts, a
> form of the whole which does not give being [*esse*]
> to each of the parts is [merely the sort of] form
> which is *composition* and *order*, as for example the
> form of a house: and such a form is an *accidental*
> form.[89] But the soul is a *substantial* form; hence, it
> is necessary that it be the form and the "act," not
> merely of the whole, but of every part. Thus, if the
> soul withdraws, just as the thing is no longer called
> "an animal" or "a human being," save equivocally,
> the way one says such things of a *pictured* animal or
> of *the statue* of an animal, so also this is the case as
> regards a hand or an eye, or flesh and bone….[90]

In describing the accidental form as not giving
"being," Thomas means "being" in the unqualified
sense, *substantial* being. As he elsewhere says:

…the substantial form brings about being, unqualifiedly [*esse simpliciter*], and its subject is a being in potency only. The accidental form, on the other hand, does not bring about being, unqualifiedly; but rather, being such, or so much, or in some relation; for its subject is a being in act. Hence, it is clear that actuality [*actualitas*] is found by priority in the substantial form rather than in its subject; and because what is first is cause in every order, the substantial form causes being in act in its subject. But, conversely, actuality is found by priority in the subject of the accidental form rather than in the accidental form; hence, the actuality of the accidental form is caused by the actuality of the subject.[91]

Thus, as Thomas indicates, the parts of the house already have actuality in themselves, and the form whereby they are a house is accidental form. This point, just in itself, should awaken a realization of the unity of a substance as such, a unity quite different from that of a machine.

When Thomas speaks of the "whole" soul, he means primarily the intrinsic perfection of the form whereby it gives substantial being.[92] Thus, it is not surprising that the whole soul must be in every part of the entity which is one as to entity. Secondarily, he has in mind that the soul, the one simple principle, is the source of the multiplicity of powers, for example, hearing, seeing, understanding, etc. Obviously, the soul in that way is in the ocular organs as to one power, sight, and in the auditory organs as to a different power, that of hearing. Thus, as to power, one "part" of the soul is in one part of the body, another in another.

However, the doctrine that the whole essential perfection of the soul is in every part of the living thing could lead to the idea that any part of the animal is an animal. Thomas corrects this misapprehension by presenting the *whole* organized body as the *proper perfectible item* corresponding to the soul as source of perfection.

THE DIFFERENCE BETWEEN FORM AND *ESSE*

Thus far I have stressed the difficulty that philosophers had in focusing on form, as well as the ultimate success that we see in Aristotle and St. Thomas. Such success is preserved only by constantly revisiting the battle over being.[93] The first thing that needs to be overcome is the temptation to look for being, as regards its most evident appearance to us, elsewhere than in the dog, the cat, the human being, and, in general, elsewhere than in sensible, generable and corruptible substances.[94]

Once we have our attention fixed on the "faces" that beings offer to our minds, these shining lights that beings are by virtue of their forms,[95] we can go on to explore the rest of St. Thomas's statement about the divinity of form. Because it is through form that a thing is a being in act, form is revealed as a participation by way of likeness of the divine nature, which is the subsisting act of being. Since, with Thomas, we affirm the distinction between a creaturely form and its act of being,[96] we might be tempted to see the likeness between God, the subsisting act of being, and the creature *merely* in function of the creature's act of being. We must not be content with this. We must also see the relation between the creature's substantial form and the divine act of being. To do so, we must exhibit the *kinship* between form and act of being within the creature. There is a continuity, as to *exemplar* causality, to be seen stretching from God as the subsisting act of being *both* to the creaturely form and to creaturely act of being.[97]

Thomas teaches, in the very text with which we began, that form gives being; form is the principle of being. "Each thing just to this extent is in act, inasmuch as it has form." One can easily illustrate this, as I do,[98] with three-letter English words. Take A, C, and T. If they are ordered as CAT, we have one word, and if as ACT, we have another word. The letters taken individually are materials, and when order, that is, form, is given to the matter, a word actually is, or has being.

So considering the situation one could call the form itself the "being" of the resulting thing, and that is exactly how Aristotle speaks in *Metaphysics* 8:

> Clearly, then, the word "is" [*to esti*] has just as
> many meanings; a thing *is* a threshold because it
> lies in such and such a position, and its being [*to einai*] means its lying in that position, while being
> ice means its having been solidified in such and
> such a way.[99]

As St. Thomas notes, "being" in such a text refers
to the proper intelligible character of the thing.
We read:

> [Aristotle] says, first, that because the aforemen-
> tioned differences are constitutive of the things
> spoken of above, it is evident that the "being"
> [*ipsum esse*] of the aforementioned things is said
> in as many ways as there are differences. For the
> difference completes the definition signifying the
> being [*esse*] of the thing. For such an item is a
> threshold because it is so positioned. And thus its
> being so positioned is its being [*esse ipsius*], that is,
> its proper intelligible character [*propria eius ratio*].
> And similarly, the being of ice is the very having
> been so solidified.[100]

I point this out, not only to recall that Thomas
himself indicates here and elsewhere this use of
the word "*esse*,"[101] but also to insist that there is
good reason for such usage, and that it reflects the
intimacy of the relation between the form and the

act of being, that is, the act which Thomas teaches is *not* to be identified with the form.

Not only does Thomas distinguish between form and *esse* in all caused things, but he teaches that where there is such a distinction, the form must have the ontological status of potency relative to the *esse*. The form, which is itself a perfection,[102] is perfected by the *esse*, which is "the perfection of perfections."[103] And yet, in the very same contexts we are told that the form is the principle and the cause of *esse*.[104] How can this be understood?

First, then, let us consider the distinction, the real distinction, between the form and the act of being in things caused by an efficient cause. To see this well one must see the thing as standing under a cause of its being, not merely of its becoming. Anything that has a cause of its becoming has also a cause of its being: thus, Thomas argues that the univocal cause, bringing into being something of its own kind (as in dogs causing dogs), cannot be the cause of doghood, their form or essence, and yet doghood must have a cause.[105] The cause which is merely a cause of becoming can subsequently be absent and yet the effect remain in being; the house builder, for example, who is merely a cause of becoming of the house, may die, and yet the house remain. On the other hand, the effect of a cause of being ceases to be if its cause ceases to cause.[106] Considering such dependence, it becomes clear that while both substantial form and act of being are within the thing, and most inwardly so, the form pertains to the selfhood of the thing in a way that the act of being cannot so pertain.

In the situation where one thing is the cause of being of another, the cause must have a higher, more noble form or nature than the effect.[107] This is so precisely because to be cause of being, one must be cause of form as such.[108] It is, indeed, the measure of this superiority of the nature of the cause over the nature of the effect that renders visible the difference between the form of the effect and its act of being.

In the modeling procedure I use, I sometimes speak of a paper hat changing into a paper airplane, the new form giving new being to the matter. Now, this tends to be merely the exhibition of a cause of *becoming*. The better model is my primitive Wheel of Fortune game, wooden letters held up manually by a human being. The words displayed are three-letter English words, and the letter supply is T, A, and C. If *the person who must hold up the letters* (and this is essential to the situation) holds up ACT, we have one word, and if she holds up CAT we have another word. However, if *she lets go* of the wooden letters, there is no word. The *order* of the letters is intrinsic to the situation, but the letters retain that order only under the *influence* of the holder. That person, the efficient cause, controls the actual existence of the word, an existence *which comes along with and through the order given to the letters.* The word is a word as having the order in the letters. The order in the letters pertains to the word's "self," but the act of being of the word, while in the word, pertains to the nature *proper* to the efficient cause, the higher nature, *in its very ascendancy.* Thus, while form and *esse* in a thing are in a kinship, are indeed *inseparable*, they are intelligibly distinct.

Notice that the form itself, the order of the letters, is not viewed as in itself foreign to the agent. Rather, the order is seen as flowing from the mind of the human being, and pertains to the wealth of being of the agent. It constitutes the means by which the agent shares the act of being.[109] This aspect of the situation is best seen by considering the *causal* role attributed to the form.

FORM AND *ESSE* AKIN: FORM AS CAUSE OF *ESSE*

That the form in the effect is a likeness of the act of being of the cause is something we need to show. It goes along with its having likeness or kinship with its own act of being. What is this "kinship" of which I speak? The form is not merely juxtaposed with the contribution of the efficient cause of being. Rather the cause of being gives the thing form precisely as the thing's *mode of cooperation with that cause*, aiming at the *goal* of the cause, actual being (*DP* 7.2 *ad* 10). We see this in the form's effect, self-maintenance, which it produces under the influence of the agent (the power of the form, its "*virtus essendi*," is flowing from the agent).[110]

Thus Thomas assures us:

> ...form, which is a part of the thing, is a likeness of the first agent, flowing from it. Hence, all forms are traced back to the first agent as to an exemplar principle.[111]

And considering the hierarchy of forms in reality, he says:

> ...according to the Philosopher, even in formal causes priority and posteriority are to be found; hence, nothing prevents one form being formed by participation in another form; and thus God himself, who is simply the act of being, is in a way *the form of all the subsisting forms* that participate the act of being and are not their own act of being.[112]

In keeping with this, the forms or natures of things are seen as *measures* of creaturely participation in the divine nature:

> The proper nature of each thing has its standing inasmuch as it participates the divine perfection in some particular measure. Thus, God would not perfectly know himself if he did not know the

way his own perfection is participable by others,
nor would he know perfectly the very nature of
being if he did not know all the *apportionments*
of being.[113]

This portioning out of being is seen in the form
in its role of self-maintenance. This is the "power"
of the form, the power to be, *virtus essendi*.[114]
It is affirmed by Thomas that the form is the
divine instrument with respect to the being in
the thing:

God causes in us natural *esse* by creation, without
the mediation of any efficient cause, but nevertheless through the mediation of a formal cause:
because natural form is the principle of natural
esse.[115]

Now, there is no real difference between the effect
of creation and the effect of conservation.[116] The
form, just as it mediates creation, mediates the
divine influence which conserves the creature
throughout its existence. As Thomas says:

…the act of being accompanies the form of the
creature, supposing nevertheless God's influence,
just as illumination follows upon the transparency
of the air, supposing the influence of the sun.[117]

Divine influence makes possible the causal role of
the form. As we read in a passage concerning the
causal role of the virtue of charity:

> ...Charity operates formally. Now, the efficacy of form is in function of the power of the agent which introduces the form [into the thing]. And therefore the fact that charity is not vanity [unlike other creatures], but rather brings about an infinite effect inasmuch as it conjoins the soul to God by giving it righteousness, demonstrates the infinity of the divine power, which is the author of charity.[118]

In the light of this divine influence, we can see why the form of the creature—though as other than being, it is necessarily potency with respect to the act of being—is nevertheless "efficacious" with respect to that act. The situation also recalls how the agent intellect, though a participation in superior intellect, nevertheless can flow from the essence of the soul as do the other powers. Thomas teaches:

> ...since the essence of the soul is immaterial, created by the supreme intellect, nothing prevents the power that is participated from the supreme intellect, [the power] by which [the soul] abstracts from matter, from proceeding from [the soul's] essence, just as the other powers.[119]

ESSE AS MOST FORMAL OF ALL

It will be a help for us at this point to call attention to the doctrine of the act of being as "most formal" in things, a view that confirms the placing of both the creaturely act of being and the creaturely form in a continuity with the divine act of being as first in the order of forms.

While in created things the form and the act of being are really distinct but inseparable from each other, the act of being is presented by St. Thomas as "most formal." That this is not a mere manner of speaking can be seen from the way it figures in the argument for divine essential infinity in *Summa theologiae* 1. There the point is first made that there is an infinity which pertains to form as such, an infinity standing on the side of perfection, in contrast to the infinity pertaining to matter and imperfection. The form meant is thus the familiar item contrasted with matter. In direct argumentative line with this, *esse* is presented as *most* formal, and God, as *esse subsistens*, is concluded to as infinite and perfect.[120]

In so arguing Thomas speaks of an *esse* that has *already* been presented as most formal of all. Indeed, in the discussion of God's being perfect at *ST* 1.4.1, an objector observes that God's essence had previously been shown to be *ipsum esse*, and yet, this seems to be most imperfect, since it is most common and receives the additions of everything else. Thomas replies:

> ...*ipsum esse* is most perfect of all. For it is compared to all as act; for nothing has actuality save

inasmuch as it is. Hence *ipsum esse* is the actuality
of all things, even of the very *forms*. Hence, it is
not related to other items as the receiver to the
received, but rather as the received to the receiver.
For when I say "the being of a man" or "the being
of a horse" or "[the being] of anything else whatsoever," "the being" [*ipsum esse*] is considered as
formal and received, and not as that to which being
belongs.[121]

Obviously St. Thomas is teaching us and encourag-
ing us to consider the act of being as most actual
in the line that we already see in the forms of
things, something in the formal order transcending other forms.

This is in keeping with *ens* or *habens esse* as the
proper effect of the highest cause,[122] *esse* being
the deepest influence of all within things. Thus, a
little later in *ST* 1, in speaking of the divine will
as all-encompassing, Thomas argues:

    ...since the effect is conformed to the agent in
    function of its [the effect's] own form, the same
    intelligible situation [*ratio*] obtains among effi-
    cient causes as is found in the formal causes. Now,
    the situation among forms is such that, though
    something can be without some particular form,
    nevertheless nothing can be without *the universal
    form*: for there can be a thing which is not a man
    or a living thing, but there cannot be something
    which is not *a being* [*ens*]. Hence, the same situa-
    tion must obtain among efficient causes....[123]

And Thomas goes on to relate the divine will, the most universal efficient cause, to that most universal form, expressed by "*ens.*"

So also, in giving his conception of the history of human knowledge of cosmic or universal causal dependence, Thomas in *De Potentia* 3.5 presents the earliest stage as thinking of all forms as accidental forms; the second stage has philosophers begin to consider substantial forms to some extent. He tells us:

> …later philosophers began to consider in some measure substantial forms; nevertheless they did not arrive at the knowledge of *universal things* [*universalium*], but their entire focus was on *special* forms [*formas speciales*]. And so they posited some efficient causes, but nevertheless not such as would confer *esse* on things universally [*non tamen quae universaliter rebus esse conferrent*], but such as would bring matter to this or that form [*ad hanc vel ad illam formam*]….[124]

The limitation of these thinkers is such that matter must remain outside the causal field. The third stage is then described as follows:

> But later philosophers, such as Plato, Aristotle, and their followers, arrived at the consideration of universal being itself [*ipsius esse universalis*], and so they alone presented a universal cause of things by which everything else is brought to be, as Augustine makes clear….

My interest here is in the use of a vocabulary—"special forms" precisely as contrasted with "universal being"—which clearly belongs to the doctrine of *esse* as most formal.

Let me offer one last example. In *ST* 1.4, as we have said, the discussion bears on God's perfection. The second article teaches that so perfect is God that the perfections of all things are found preexistent in him. In the body of the article there are two arguments, the second of which considers God as the subsisting act of being. It views the act of being as a formal nature comparable in that respect to such a formal nature as heat. It concludes that the subsisting act of being must contain the entire perfection of being. And it further concludes that this means that it contains the perfections of all things, because, and I quote:

> Now, the perfections of all things pertain to the perfection of being: for it is in function of this that particular things are perfect, namely, that they have being in some *measure*.[125]

The particular forms or natures of things are viewed as pertaining to the perfection that is seen in the act of being.

This is made plainer in the next article, as to whether any creature can be *similar* to God. The placing of this query in the discussion of perfection relates to the doctrine that a thing when perfect can produce something like itself.[126] Thomas explains likeness or similarity as "having *form* in common" [*communicandi in forma*], and eventually comes to the mode of community which links creatures to the creator, a *formal* community through a sort of analogy: "as being itself [*ipsum esse*] is common to all."[127]

Should we be confused? Does it seem that "*esse*" signifies an aspect of the very essence of things after all? No, rather we are invited to see special forms as belonging, in a diminished way, to the domain of existence. That is why, at the very beginning of this essay, I presented in my "beacon text" on form its role as the intrinsic active principle of preservation of existence.

Conclusion

I began by mentioning the recent controversies between evolutionary scientists and design theorists. I saw this as an argument about the origin and nature of form, and accordingly thought a reflection on form would be in order. "Form" here meant substantial form.

I took as a starting-point the teaching of both Aristotle and Thomas Aquinas that form is something divine in things. I called attention to the difficulty scientists seem to have had with form, as seen from our knowledge of earliest Western thought. I wished to suggest that the current arguments are not something new. On the one hand, we live in the world of nature, the world of dogs and cats and human beings. On the other hand, the changes that take place in that world suggest analyses that tend to locate the being of things in some already given fundamental stuff or stuffs.

My judgment is that the Socratic question, "what makes one thing one?" rightly leads to the focus on form, and that Aristotle's hylomorphism is, as Gilson said, "evident," but, as Aristotle said, is at the summit of theoretical thought, requiring the solving of a most astonishingly difficult problem, that is, how to conceive of unqualified coming to be and ceasing to be in nature. Aristotle thus saves the primacy in being of the dog, the cat, and the human being, as contrasted with any mere particle or bundle theory of such things. However, the human mind is such, depending as it does on the data of sense and imagination, that it is easily seduced into a reduction of our familiar natural substances to mere epiphenomena. There will always be a battle about the being of things.

I have gone on to offer considerations of the fundamental ontology of created reality as presented by St. Thomas that, as I hope, help us to view the particular substantial forms of things as in a continuum with the divine act of being. In so doing, I have aimed to present a most "existential" conception of substantial form. It truly is the principle of the act of being of the thing. It is so, under divine efficacy.

Does the metaphysician have anything to say relevant to the battle between the design theorists and the evolutionary scientists? On the one hand, what I have been suggesting places form in the realm of products of the divine mind. The forms of things have a unity which we rightly associate with mind.

Once one recognizes the need to trace the forms to the divine mind, there remains the entire question of how the actual forms which we witness in things get to be there. A world containing created causes may house secondary sources of form. They may be so by their own natural power conferred by the creator,[128] or they may be so as mere instruments of the creator obtaining intelligent results from what, at the level of secondary causality, is chance.[129]

Darwin actually suggested something like this latter situation at one point in his life, contending that it did more honor to the creator than having the creator directly involved in everything. He thought this agreed with St. Thomas's view that secondary causality gives honor to the creator.[130] In fact, what Darwin suggested would not be true secondary causality of the forms, but mere *per accidens* causality of them, things actually doing something else and happening to hit upon forms.

Thomas thought that God was honored by true secondary causality being granted to his creatures, and this at a very universal level.[131]

In Thomas's time, it was thought that the celestial bodies were incorruptible and of a higher order of corporeal existence than sublunary or terrestrial, corporeal reality. Thus, they were theorized to be intermediate causes, themselves acting under still more powerful created spirits.[132] Perhaps some day we will have discovered enough about corporeal reality to provide candidates for such universal causality under God. What is certain is that the forms of things require a divine origin, even if they continue to appear in what may seem a random way.

I have not stressed in my presentation the line of argument for the existence of a creator God. I did mention the need for causal hierarchy. That needs only the added premise that one cannot go to infinity in such hierarchy to establish the existence of God, indeed, as the subsisting act of being.[133] To attempt to account for the forms of things entirely by chance and material necessity amounts to seeing the origin of all things in mere potency, like the theologian poets and primitive cosmologists criticized by Aristotle.[134]

NOTES

1. Thomas Aquinas, *In octo libros Physicorum Aristotelis expositio*, ed. P. M. Maggiolo (Turin-Rome: Marietti, 1950) [=*CP: Commentary on Aristotle's Physics*] 1.15 (12):

   Then, there where [Aristotle] says: "But about the principle, etc.," since he has already excluded the errors concerning matter and privation, it would seem that it remains for him to exclude the errors and difficulties concerning form. Some people, indeed, posited separate forms, that is, the Ideas, which they traced back to one primary Idea. And so he says that concerning the formal principle, whether it is one or many, and how many, and which they are, it pertains to primary philosophy to determine, and it is set aside until that time: *because form is the principle of being, and being as such is the subject of primary philosophy;* but matter and privation are principles of changeable being, which is considered by the natural philosopher. Nevertheless, there will be determination concerning natural and corruptible forms in what follows in this [present] doctrine.

2. Cf. Thomas Aquinas, *Summa theologiae* (Ottawa: Institutum Studiorum Medievalium Ottaviense, 1953) [=*ST*] 1.3.2: God must be "*primo et per se forma,*" "*per essentiam suam forma.*" See Thomas Aquinas, *De immortalitate animae, ad* 17: "form" and "act" are among the things predicated analogically of diverse things: "…forma et actus et huiusmodi sunt de hiis que analogice predicantur de diversis" (ed. Kennedy, p. 222); cf. Leonard A. Kennedy, "A New Disputed Question of St. Thomas Aquinas on the Immortality of the Soul," *Archives d'histoire doc-*

trinale et littéraire du moyen âge 45 (1978) 205-208
(introduction) and 209-223 (text).

3 Étienne Gilson, *D'Aristote à Darwin et retour: Essai
   sur quelques constantes de la biophilosophie* (Paris: Vrin,
   1971); *From Aristotle to Darwin and Back Again: A
   Journey in Final Causality, Species, and Evolution*,
   trans. John Lyon (Notre Dame, IN: University of
   Notre Dame Press, 1984).

4 Gilson, *D'Aristote*, pp. 33-34:

   Aristotle found finality in nature so evident that he asked
   himself how his predecessors could have failed to see, and
   even worse, denied its presence there. Their error was
   explained, in his eyes, because they erred concerning the
   notions of essence and substance [*Parts of Animals* 1.1].
   The subsequent history of philosophy should confirm
   the accuracy of his diagnosis because as long as the
   Aristotelian notion of substance as unity of a matter and
   a form survived, that of finality remained undisputed,
   but as soon as in the seventeenth century Bacon and
   Descartes /34/ denied the notion of substantial form
   (form that constitutes a substance by its union with
   a matter), that of final cause became inconceivable.
   Indeed, substance as defined by its form is the end of
   generation. What remained, once the form was excluded,
   was the extended matter, or rather extension itself, which
   is the object of geometry and is susceptible only to purely
   mechanical modifications. Descartes submitted to mech-
   anism the entire domain of living beings, including the
   human body. The celebrated Cartesian theory of "animal
   machines," which rightly astonished La Fontaine, illus-
   trates this point perfectly [my translation].

5 Cf. Étienne Gilson, Jacques Maritain, *Deux appro-
   ches de l'être: Correspondance 1923-1971*, ed. Géry

Prouvost (Paris: Vrin, 1991), pp. 247-248 (letter of
Maritain, Sept. 3, 1971).

6 Cf. *ibid.*, p. 250 (letter of Gilson, Sept. 8, 1971). He
is speaking of "la science moderne:"

> Ce qui nous en sépare irréparablement est la notion
> aristotélicienne (et de sens commun) de la Forme Sub-
> stantielle…. Descartes en a dépeuplé la nature. On ne
> comprend plus rien depuis qu'on a oublié la grande
> parole d'Aristote, qu'il n'y a "aucune partie d'un animal
> qui soit purement matérielle ou purement immatérielle."
> Ce n'est pas le mot philosophie, c'est le mot nature qui
> nous sépare de nos contemporains. Comme je n'espère
> pas les convaincre de la vérité (pourtant évidente) de
> l'hylémorphisme, je ne crois pas possible de leur proposer
> notre hypothèse comme scientifiquement valide.

For the statement of Aristotle, cf. *Parts of Animals*
1.3 (643a25).

7 In Thomas Aquinas, *In duodecim libros Metaphysicorum Aristotelis expositio*, ed. M.-R. Cathala and
R. Spiazzi (Turin-Rome: Marietti, 1950) [=*CM*:
Commentary on Aristotle's Metaphysics], 7.2, Aquinas
sees the primary interest of Aristotle as bearing upon
substance in the sense of subject (n. 1274), and that,
in the subject, it is the substantial form that is to be
the chief target of investigation (1296). St. Thomas
also speaks of it as the particular form [*forma particu-
laris*] (1276-77). It is this which is presented at the
very beginning, albeit in barest outline, as the cause
of *ens*: matter is not constituted as a being actually
[*ens actu*] except through form; thus, form is the
"because of which [*propter quod*]" (1278).

8 Aristotle, *Physics* 1.9 (192a17-19), trans. R. P. Hardie
and R. K. Gaye, in *The Works of Aristotle*, ed. W. D.

Ross (Oxford: Clarendon Press, 1908-1952), vol. 2.
Cf. Aristotle, *Physics* 1.7-9, for the general presentation of the principles.

9 Aquinas, *CP* 1.15 (7 [135]):

...forma est quoddam divinum et optimum et appetibile. Divinum quidem est, quia omnis forma est
quaedam participatio similitudinis divini esse, quod est
actus purus: unumquodque enim in tantum est actu in
quantum habet formam. Optimum autem est, quia actus
est perfectio potentiae et bonum eius: et per consequens
sequitur quod sit appetibile, quia unumquodque appetit
suam perfectionem.

Oddly enough, in Étienne Gilson, *Elements of
Christian Philosophy* (Garden City, N.Y.: Doubleday,
1960), p. 154, Gilson speaks of the last principle used
by Thomas in the above: "each thing has appetite for
its own perfection," as "an appeal to psychological
experience." It is, rather, a statement reflecting the
doctrine that nature is a cause that acts for an end;
cf., for example, *ST* 1.60.1 and 3.

Cf. Thomas Aquinas, *Summa contra gentiles*,
ed. C. Pera et al. (Turin-Rome: Marietti, 1961)
[=*SCG*] 3.97.3:

Ex diversitate autem formarum sumitur ratio ordinis
rerum. Cum enim forma sit secundum quam res habet
esse; res autem quaelibet secundum quod habet esse,
accedat ad similitudinem Dei, qui est ipsum suum esse
simplex: necesse est quod forma nihil sit aliud quam
divina similitudo participata in rebus; unde conveni-
enter Aristoteles, in I *Physic.*, de forma loquens, dicit
quod est divinum quoddam et appetibile. [Now, the
rationale of the order of things is seen from the diversity
of forms. For, since form is that according to which the

thing has being, and any thing according as it has being
approaches likeness to God, who is his own simple act
of being, it is necessary that form be nothing else but a
divine likeness participated by things; hence, Aristotle
says fittingly, in *Physics* 1, speaking of form, that it is
something divine in things.]

Cf. Thomas Aquinas, *In Aristotelis libros De caelo et
mundo, De generatione et corruptione, Meteorologico-
rum expositio*, ed. R. Spiazzi (Turin-Rome: Marietti,
1952), *In De caelo* 3.2 (552 [2]):

Etsi enim de his quae cadunt sub generatione et corruptione sit aliqua scientia, hoc non est nisi inquantum
in eis est aliquid ingenitum et incorruptibile, secundum
participationem illarum naturarum, quae secundum se
sunt ingenitae et incorruptibiles: cognoscuntur enim
secundum suas formas, forma autem est quoddam divinum in rebus, inquantum est quaedam participatio
primi actus. [For if there is some science concerning
those things which are subject to generation and corruption, this is only inasmuch as in them there is something
ungenerated and incorruptible, in virtue of participation
in those natures which are ungenerated and incorruptible
in themselves; for [such things] are known in function
of their forms: but form is something divine in things,
inasmuch as it is some participation in the first act.]

10 I say "to matter," merely because in the context of
    Physics 1 the discussion is about the hylomorphic
    doctrine. Thomas does not limit the doctrine of form
    giving being to the case of material things. Thus we
    read, at *CM* 3.4 (384):

    …[Aristotle] determines in Book 4 that this science [that
    is, metaphysics] considers *ens* ["that which is"] inasmuch
    as it is *ens*: and so it belongs to it to consider the primary

substances, and not to natural science, because above
mobile substance there are other substances. But every
substance either is *ens* through itself, if it is form alone,
or else, if it is composed out of matter and form, it is *ens*
through its own form; hence, inasmuch as this science
undertakes to consider *ens*, it considers most of all the
formal cause.

11 Cf. *ST* 1.3.1 (the second argument in the corpus,
basing itself on the Fourth Way in 1.2.3), together
with 1.3.2 (the first argument in the corpus). Notice
that in *ST* 1.13.11, on "*qui est*" as the most proper
name of God, it is *esse* as the *form* or essence of God
which is appealed to (in the first argument in the
corpus).

12 *The Concise Oxford Dictionary of Current English*,
edd. H. W. Fowler and F. G. Fowler, 5th ed., revised
by E. McIntosh (Oxford: Oxford University Press,
1964), *ad loc.*

13 Thomas Aquinas, *Scriptum super libros Sententia-
rum*, ed. P. Mandonnet and M. Moos (Paris: Lethiel-
leux, 1929-1947) [=*Sent.*] 1.28.2.1:

> …non dicimus quod qui imitatur aliquem in albedine,
> sit imago illius; sed qui imitatur in *figura*, quae est *proxi-
> mum signum et expressum speciei et naturae.* Videmus
> enim diversarum specierum in animalibus diversas esse
> figuras.

One should not think such a sign is demonstrative.
Cf. *Sent.* 4.11.2.2A obj. 3 and *ad* 3 (pp. 464 [171]
and 467 [186]): Shape is only a sign.

14 Notice that such words as "idea" and "species" relate
etymologically to seeing and the visible. Accordingly,
in Thomas Aquinas, *Super Epistolas s. Pauli lectura*,
ed. R. Cai (Turin: Marietti, 1953), we find Thomas

commenting, at *Super Primam epistolam b. Pauli ad Timotheum lectura* 6.3:

Lux in sensibilibus est principium videndi; unde illud quo aliquid cognoscitur quocumque modo, dicitur lux. Unumquodque autem cognoscitur per suam formam, et secundum quod est actu. Unde quantum habet de forma et actu, tantum habet de luce. Res ergo, quae sunt actus quidam, sed non purus, lucentia sunt, sed non lux. Sed divina essentia, quae est actus purus, est ipsa lux. *Iohan.* 1.8: non erat ille lux, etc.. Deus autem habitat apud se, et haec lux est inaccessibilis, id est, non visibilis oculo carnis, sed intelligibilis. [Light in [the domain of] sensible things is the principle of seeing: hence, that by virtue of which something is known in any way is called "light." Now, each thing is known through its own form and inasmuch as it is in act. Hence, in the measure in which something has form and act, to that extent it has light. Thus, things which are acts, indeed, but not pure [act] are lucent, but are not light. But the divine essence, which is pure act, is light itself. Cf. *John* 1.8: "he was not the light, etc." But God lives in his own [domain], and this light is inaccessible, that is, is not visible to the fleshly eye, but intelligible.]

15 Aristotle, *Metaphysics* 7.3 (1028b36-1029a9), trans. W. D. Ross, in *The Works of Aristotle*, vol. 8.

16 While the Ross translation, following the medieval Latin, regularly translates "*ousia*" as "substance," a more imitative approach would use the word "entity," a Latin-derived term having the verb "to be" as root, and the same sort of abstract ending as has the Greek.

17 Aristotle even says that the form is more a being than is the composite; he gives as argument for this

62 Lawrence Dewan

the fact that the composite contains the matter. In other words, just as form is more of a being than matter, so also the form is the source of whatever being one attributes to the composite. Nevertheless, I cannot help thinking of St. Thomas's remarks elsewhere in *CM* 7.6 (1386):

Matter and form…are not substances, except insofar as they are the principles of composite substance.

Also, in *CM* 8.1, in explaining the division of substance into matter, form, and composite, and their status as substances, the composite appears to get the primary role:

But the composite out of these is said to be substance as *separable unqualifiedly,* that is, capable of existing by itself separately in reality; *and of it alone* there is *generation and corruption* (1687).

The reference to generation and corruption is a way of pointing out that this is the thing which is, in the primary sense of "is." Cf. *CM* 7.1 (1256) and 6.2 (1179); also 4.2 (551-552).

18 See Thomas Aquinas, *De substantiis separatis* c. 7, ll. 47-52, in *Opera omnia: iussu impensaque, Leonis XIII. P.M. edita* (Rome: Commissio Leonina, 1882–), vol. 40:

Manifestum est autem quod cum ens per potentiam et actum dividatur, quod actus est potentia perfectior et magis habet de ratione essendi; non enim simpliciter esse dicimus quod est in potentia, sed solum quod est actu. [It is evident that, since that-which-is is divided by potency and act, act is more perfect than potency and has *more* of the intelligible character of *being*: for we do not say "is," unqualifiedly, of that which is in potency, but rather of that which is in act.]

While all five ways to God (*ST* 1.2.3) are metaphysical, the Fourth is primary in this regard. All reduce to the priority of act over potency, and so to the "*magis*" and "*minus*" as regards the *ratio essendi*, explicitly presented in the Fourth Way.

19 Thomas Aquinas, *Sentencia libri De anima* 2.7, ll. 176-181, in *Opera omnia*, vol. 45.1, concerning Aristotle, *De anima* 2.4 (415a13).

20 Aristotle, *Metaphysics* 7.17 (1041b26): "*aition ge tou einai*." He goes on to speak of "*ousia*" as the "first cause of being [*aition prōton tou einai*]" (1041b28).

21 Cf. Aquinas, *CM* 7.11 (1529-1532).

22 Thomas Aquinas, *De ente et essentia* c. 1, ll. 53-63, in *Opera omnia*, vol. 43. Literally, the text places essence in God "more truly," but the implication "most" is obvious.

23 *ST* 1.3.2; notice *ST* 1.42.1 *ad* 1 (264b29-33): the effects of form are, first, being, and second, operation.

24 Aristotle, *De caelo* 2.6 (288b14); see Aquinas, *In De caelo* 2.9 (375 [2]).

25 Ultimately, that premise would have to be traced to the cause of being as being. Only thus can one see that there is need, in a complete universe, for the two modes of created being, namely, incorruptible and corruptible; cf. *ST* 1.22.4 *in toto*; also 1.48.2. Cf. also Lawrence Dewan, "Thomas Aquinas and Being as a Nature," *Acta Philosophica* 12 (2003) 123-135.

26 Notice here the doctrine of "some inclination accompanying every form" (*ST* 1.80.1); cf. also *ST*

1.59.1 as seeing this all flowing from the divine will. We also have an "inclination of the matter."

27 *ST* 1-2.85.6; cf. *ST* 1.97.1.

28 Cf. *In De caelo* 2.18 (468 [11]):

> …optimum in rebus est permanentia. Quae quidem in substantiis separatis est absque omni motu; et quidquid permanentiae est in inferioribus rebus, illinc derivatur. [...what is best in things is permanence. This is found in the separate substances altogether without movement; and whatever there is of permanence in lower things is derived from them.]

29 Cf. Thomas Aquinas, *Expositio libri Posteriorum* [*Commentary on Aristotle's Posterior Analytics*] 1.37, ll. 173-187, in *Opera omnia*, vol. 1.2, commenting on Aristotle, 85b15. This passage from Thomas, echoing Aristotle, seems to me best to express the importance of the two metaphysical dimensions of the being which confronts us, the universal or specific and the individual:

> And he [Aristotle] says that if the universal is said of many in function of one intelligibility [*rationem*] and not equivocally, the universal as regards what pertains to reason [*quantum ad id quod rationis est*], that is, as regards science and demonstration, will not be less of a being [*minus ens*] than the particulars, but rather more, because the incorruptible is more of a being [*magis ens*] than the corruptible, and the universal intelligibility [*ratio universalis*] is incorruptible whereas the particulars are corruptible, with corruptibility happening to them in function of the individual principles, not in function of the intelligibility [*rationem*] of the species, which is common to all and preserved by generation. Thus, therefore, as regards what pertains to reason, universals *ARE* more

[*magis sunt*] than the particulars, but as regards natural subsistence [*quantum uero ad naturalem subsistenciam*], the particulars ARE to a greater extent [*magis sunt*], [and thus] are called "primary and principal substances."

The universal is "preserved through genera-tion" here, that is, is seen in and has being in the particulars.

30 Étienne Gilson, *Being and Some Philosophers*, 2nd ed. (Toronto: Pontifical Institute of Mediaeval Studies, 1952), p. ix.

31 *CP* 1.13 (118 [9]), quoted below at n. 64. Cf. also *ST* 1.87.1; and also *Super Ad Timoth*. 1, 6.3, in n. 14 above; also Thomas Aquinas, *Super Evangelium s. Ioannis lectura*, ed. R. Cai (Rome-Turin: Marietti, 1952), 1.4 (118):

Cum enim unumquodque manifestetur per suam for-mam et cognoscatur, omnes autem formae sint per Ver-bum, quod est ars plena rationum viventium: est ergo lumen, non solum in se, sed omnia manifestans.... [For since each thing is manifested and known through its form, and all forms are through the Word, which is the Art full of the plans of living things, therefore [the Word] is light, not merely in itself but as making all things manifest....]

32 Cf. *De substantiis separatis* c. 6, ll. 88-129. Clearly, in this explicit statement from St. Thomas about the starting-points of metaphysics, it is precisely natural substances, *per se* units, which are so des-ignated. In speaking of the subsisting thing as such, I add, St. Thomas generally refers to its "itself *having*" being, and explains that further by the expression: "subsisting in *its own* being," this in contrast to the mode of being of *inhering* accidents and forms which

cannot exist except as actually perfecting matter; such items are called "beings" not as themselves having being, but as that in function of which the composite is. Thus, we read at *ST* 1.45.4:

Fieri autem ordinatur ad esse rei. Unde illis proprie convenit fieri et creari, quibus convenit esse. Quod quidem convenit proprie subsistentibus, sive sint simplicia, sicut substantiae separatae; sive sint composita, sicut substantiae materiales. Illi enim proprie convenit esse, quod *habet* esse; et hoc est subsistens in *suo* esse. Formae autem et accidentia, et alia huiusmodi, non dicuntur entia quasi ipsa sint, sed quia eis aliquid est; ut albedo ea ratione dicitur ens, quia ea subiectum est album. [Coming to be is ordered towards the being of the thing. Hence, to those items it properly belongs to be brought into being and to be created to which it belongs to be: now, [being] properly belongs to subsisting things, whether they be simple, as in the case of the separate substance, or composite, as in the case of material substances. This is because to that item it properly belongs to be which *has* being, and this is what is subsisting in *its own* being. But [inherent] forms and accidents and other items of this order are not called "beings" as though they themselves are, but rather because in function of them something is: for example, whiteness is called "a being" for this reason, because in function of it the subject is a white thing.]

33 On identity as substantial unity, cf. Aquinas, *CM* 4.2 (561). The notion of "identity" pertains primarily to substance as substance; all such words as "self," "same," "one's own" relate to the mode of oneness proper to substance. Cf. nevertheless *CM* 7.4 (1331-1334), concerning the fact that all the categories

participate in the mode of entity proper to substance, such as being a "what" [*quid*], etc.

34 Our focal point, the substantial form, does not itself subsist save in the case of the human soul, but it is, as we shall see, the principle of the subsisting thing's subsisting. Cf. *ST* 1.29.2 *ad* 5.

35 Cf. Aristotle, *Metaph.* 1.3 (983b8-18 and 984a31-33).

36 Aristotle, *De caelo* 3.6 (305a1-4), referred to by Joseph Owens, *A History of Ancient Western Philosophy* (New York: Appleton-Century-Crofts, 1959), p. 105.

37 Translation by Owens, *ibid.*

38 Kathleen Freeman, *Ancilla to the Presocratic Philosophers* (Oxford: B. Blackwell, 1948), quoted by Owens, *History*, p. 106.

39 I do not mean to suggest that present-day particle physicists have as little experimental grounds for talking about particles as Empedocles had. On the question of the reality of fundamental particles in modern physics, cf. William A. Wallace, "Are Elementary Particles Real?" in *From a Realist Point of View: Essays on the Philosophy of Science* (Washington, D.C.: University Press of America, 1979), pp. 187-200.

40 Cf. Aristotle, *Physics* 2.8 (198b23-33).

41 On the Socratic problem, cf. Owens, *History*, pp. 165-169. Even though Aristotle tells us, at *Metaph.* 1.6 (987b1-4), that Socrates worked in the domain of ethics rather than of the natural world, Plato's account of his younger days may well be true.

42 Plato, *Phaedo* 96B, in Plato, *Euthyphro, Apology, Crito, Phaedo, Phaedrus*, trans. H. N. Fowler

68   Lawrence Dewan

(Cambridge, Mass.: Harvard University Press, 1960
[original 1914]). The passage continues:

> Or is it none of these, and does the brain furnish the sen-
> sations of hearing and sight and smell, and do memory
> and opinion arise from these, and does knowledge come
> from memory and opinion in a state of rest?

43 Plato, *Phaedo* 97B, trans. Hugh Tredennick, in *The
    Collected Dialogues of Plato*, edd. E. Hamilton and H.
    Cairns (New York: Pantheon Books, 1961):

> Nor can I now persuade myself that I understand how it
> is that things become one, nor, in short, why anything
> else comes or ceases or continues to be, according to this
> method of inquiry.

44 Thomas Aquinas, *Quaestio disputata de spiritualibus
    creaturis* 3, ll. 233-238, in *Opera omnia*, vol. 24.2:

> …unumquodque enim secundum hoc est unum secun-
> dum quod est ens. Est autem unumquodque ens actu
> per formam, siue secundum esse substantiale siue secun-
> dum esse accidentale: unde *omnis forma est actus, et per
> consequens est ratio unitatis qua aliquid est unum.* [For
> in function of this each thing is one, namely, inasmuch
> as it is a being. But each thing is a being in act through
> form, whether according to substantial being or accord-
> ing to accidental being: hence, all form is act and con-
> sequently is the principle of unity in function of which
> something is one.]

45 Plato, *Phaedo* 100Bff.; note in particular 101C,
    trans. H. Tredennick:

> You would loudly proclaim that you know of no other
> way in which any given object can come into being
> except by participation in the reality peculiar [*tēs idias*

ousias] to its appropriate universal, and that in the cases
which I have mentioned you recognize no other cause
for the coming into being of two than participation
in duality, and that whatever is to become two must
participate in this, and whatever is to become one must
participate in unity.

46 Aristotle, *Metaph.* 1.10 (993a11-16), trans. W. D.
Ross:

> It is evident, then, even from what we have said before,
> that all men seem to seek the causes named in the *Phys-
> ics*, and that we cannot name any beyond these; but
> they seek these vaguely; and though in a sense they
> have all been described before, in a sense they have not
> been described at all. For the earliest philosophy is, on
> all subjects, like one who lisps, since it is young and in
> its beginnings.

47 Aristotle, *Metaph.* 1.7 (988a34-b1).

48 Aristotle, *Metaph.* 1.8 (988b28-29).

49 Cf. *Phaedo* 81B-82B and 83C-D; note especially
the criticism of Plato (along with others) by Aristotle
at *De anima* 1.3 (407b22-25), trans. J. A. Smith, in
The Works of Aristotle, vol. 3:

> All, however, that these thinkers do is to describe the
> specific characteristics of the soul; they do not try to
> determine anything about the body which is to contain
> it, as if it were possible, as in the Pythagorean myths,
> that any soul could be clothed upon with any body – an
> absurd view, for each body seems to have a form and
> shape of its own. It is as absurd as to say that the art of
> carpentry could embody itself in flutes; each art must
> use its tools, each soul its body.

50 Cf. Aquinas, *Sentencia libri De anima* 2.1, ll. 366-
    392, commenting on Aristotle, 412b6:

> And this is what [Aristotle] says: that one ought not to
> ask if out of the soul and the body something one is
> effected, just as neither does one raise a question con-
> cerning the wax and the shape, nor generally concerning
> any matter and the form pertaining to the matter; for it
> has been shown in *Metaphysics* 8 that form is united just
> by virtue of itself to the matter, as its act; and it is the
> same thing for the matter to be united to the form, as for
> the matter to be in act. And this is also what [Aristotle]
> says here, that though "a being" and "something one" are
> said in many ways, such as of a being in potency and of
> a being in act, that which properly is a being and one is
> act; for just as a being in potency is not "a being" in the
> unqualified sense, but [merely] in a way, so also it is not
> "something one" in an unqualified sense, but [merely] in
> a way: for something is called "something one" inasmuch
> as [it is called] "a being." And therefore, just as the body
> has being [*esse*] through the soul, as through form, so
> also it is united to the soul immediately, inasmuch as
> the soul is the form of the body. However, inasmuch as
> [the soul] is a mover, nothing prevents something being
> an intermediary, inasmuch as one part [of the body] is
> moved by the soul through the mediation of another.

51 Cf. Aristotle, *De anima* 2.4 (415a13); Aquinas,
    Sentencia libri De anima 2.7, ll. 176-181; see above
    at n. 19.

52 Cf. Aquinas, *CM* 7.9 (1469-1470), concerning
    Aristotle at 7.10 (1034b32 ff); cf. Aquinas, *ST* 1.85.1
    ad 2. See also Lawrence Dewan, *Form and Being*
    (Washington, D.C.: Catholic University of America
    Press, 2006), ch. 8.

53 Matter and form "...*tēn akrotatēn echei thean;*" that is, they are "at the very apex of speculative thought" (Aristotle, *The Physics* 4.2 [209b18-21], trans. Philip Wicksteed and Francis M. Cornford [Cambridge, Mass.: Harvard University Press, 1934]);" "*altissimam habent speculationem*" in the translation commented upon by Thomas. Cf. Aquinas, *CP* 4.3 (428 [7]):

> ...tam materia quam forma habent *altissimam speculationem et difficilem*; et non est facile etiam cognoscere unum eorum sine altero. [...both matter and form require a lofty and difficult inquiry, and it is also not easy to consider one of them without the other.]

54 Plato, *Timaeus* 49A-52D.

55 Aristotle, *Physics* 1.9 (191b35-192a17).

56 Aristotle, *Metaph.* 7.3 (1029a33-34); cf. Aquinas, *CM* 7.2 (1297-98); and cf. Aristotle, *ibid.* 7.2 (1028b8-15), and Aquinas, *CM* 7.1 (1263-64 and 1269).

57 *Sent* 2.34.1.2 *ad* 5 (ed. Mandonnet, p. 878):

> ...corruption and generation, though they are always conjoined, nevertheless are not essentially identical, but [only] through association; this is clear from their termini, from which movements and changes are specified: for the terminus of generation is the form, because it is a change [going] towards being, whereas the terminus of corruption is the privation, because it is a change [going] towards not being. Now, the form of one thing and the privation of another, such as the form of fire and the privation of air, are indeed one as to subject but differ in intelligible character. And therefore, also, that which corrupts and generates [something] does not have it from the same [root] that it generates and corrupts; but by

the fact that it introduces its form, it generates; and thus it generates inasmuch as it is a being. But by the fact that its form is necessarily conjoined to the privation of another form, it corrupts [something]. Hence it is clear that something corrupts by the fact that it has privation or is "non-being;" and that is why Dionysius says that it belongs essentially to the good to generate and to preserve, and to the bad to corrupt; hence, it does not follow that the bad precisely as bad is something.

58 Cf. *CM* 8.1 (1689); as St. Thomas says:

From this argument of Aristotle it is apparent that substantial generation and corruption are the starting-point for coming to the knowledge of prime matter.

59 Cf. Aristotle using "you" as the key to substance, as contrasted with the accidental: for you to be musical is not for you to be you, or for you to be. Cf. Aquinas, *CM* 7.3 (1309) on Aristotle, *Metaph.* 7.4 (1029b13-15): ..."to be musical" is not "for you to be."

60 *SCG* 2.17.4:

In omni mutatione vel motu oportet esse aliquid aliter se habens nunc et prius: hoc enim ipsum nomen mutationis ostendit. [In every change or movement it is necessary that there be something which is otherwise now than before: for this the very word "change" shows.]

Cf. also *ST* 1.45.2 *ad* 2; Thomas Aquinas, *Quaestiones disputatae de potentia Dei* 3.2, in *Quaestiones disputatae*, ed. P. Bazzi et al. (Turin-Rome: Marietti, 1953), vol. 2 [=*DP*]; Thomas Aquinas, *Compendium theologiae* 1.99, in *Opera omnia*, vol. 42. Concerning the premise that a subject must underlie all natural production, Thomas notes at *CP* 1.12 (107 [10]) that Aristotle in *Physics* 1 employs a mere induction, surveying types of change. Thomas says that this is because it pertains to metaphysics to provide the reason, and he refers us, seemingly, to *Metaphysics* 7 for this reason. Fr. Maggiolo refers us to *CM* 7.6, where, indeed, at n. 1388 a relevant discussion occurs. However, that discussion itself sends us to an earlier passage where it has already been seen that matter is in potency to the forms and to the privations; this seems to be a reference to *CM* 7.2 (1285-1290). Now, there, Thomas sends us back to the *Physics*! It is possible that the reference in *CP* to the *Metaphysics* should be to book 12. At *CM* 12.2 (2432-33) Thomas presents Aristotle at *Metaph.* 12.2 (1069b15), where he gives the argument for unqualified coming to be, in terms of being as divided by act and potency. This is an explicitly metaphysical account of the subject underlying form and privation. Indeed, the account corresponds to what St. Thomas mentions at *CP* 1.14 (126-127 [7-8]), commenting on Aristotle at *Phys.* 1.8 (191b27-29), though Thomas understandably there sends us to *Metaph.* 9.

61 *CM* 7.2 (1286):

...it is necessary that the subject of change and motion be other, speaking essentially *[per se loquendo],* than either of the termini of motion, as is proved in *Physics* 1. Hence, since matter is the first subject standing under not merely motions, which are according to quality and quantity and the other accidents, but even [under] the changes which are according to substance, it is necessary that matter be other, according to its own essence, than all substantial forms and their privations, which are the termini of generation and corruption; and not

merely that it be other than quantity and quality and
the other accidents.

62 Thomas does not hesitate to pinpoint that being.
Cf., for example, *Sent.* 2.1.1.1 *ad* 5:

> Ad quintum dicendum, quod quamvis Deus nullo modo
> sit materia, nihilominus tamen *ipsum esse quod materia
> habet imperfectum, prout dicitur ens in potentia,* habet a
> Deo, et reducitur in ipsum sicut in principium. Similiter
> et *forma*, quae pars est rei, *est similitudo agentis primi
> fluens ab ipso.* Unde *omnes formae reducuntur in primum
> agens sicut in principium exemplare.* Et sic patet quod est
> unum primum principium simpliciter, quod est primum
> agens, et exemplar, et finis ultimus. [...though God is
> in no way [identifiable with] matter, nevertheless the
> imperfect being which matter has, inasmuch as it is
> called "a being in potency," it has from God, and [thus]
> is traced back to him as to a principle. Similarly, also, the
> form which is a part of the thing is a likeness of the first
> agent, flowing forth from him. Thus, all forms are traced
> back to the first agent as to the exemplar principle.]

Cf. also *Sent* 1.36.2.3 *ad* 2 (ed. Mandonnet, pp.
844-845):

> ...since prime matter is from God, it is necessary that
> its idea be in some way [*aliqualiter*] in God; and in the
> way that *esse* is attributed to it, in just that way an idea
> in God is attributed to it: because every *esse*, inasmuch
> as it is perfect, is exemplarily derived from the divine
> *esse.* But perfect *esse* does not belong to matter just in
> itself [*in se*], but only according as it is in the composite.
> In itself, however, it has imperfect *esse*, according to the
> ultimate grade of being [*secundum ultimum gradum
> essendi*], which is being in potency [*esse in potentia*]. And
> so it only has the perfect intelligibility [*rationem*] of an

idea according as it is in the composite, because so taken, God confers upon it perfect *esse*. But considered in itself, it has in God the imperfect character [*rationem*] of an idea; this is to say, the divine essence is imitable by the composite according to perfect *esse*, by matter according to imperfect *esse*, but by privation in no way....

63 Cf. Aquinas, *CM* 2.1 (280) on Aristotle, *Metaph.* 2.1 (993b7-8): matter, motion, and time are difficult to know because of their intrinsic mode of being, namely, imperfect being.

64 Aquinas, *CP* 1.13 (118 [9]), concerning Aristotle at *Phys.* 1.7 (191a8).

65 Aristotle says, *De generatione et corruptione* 1.3 (317b18-20), trans. Harold H. Joachim, in *The Works of Aristotle*, vol. 2:

...it is extraordinarily difficult [*thaumastēn aporian*] to see how there can be "unqualified coming-to-be" (whether we suppose it to occur out of what potentially "is" [*ek dunamei ontos*], or in some other way), and we must recall this problem for further examination.

See Thomas Aquinas, *In De generatione et corruptione* 1.6 (49 [8]), in Aquinas, *In Aristotelis libros De caelo, De generatione*:

...because even after the preceding determination there still looms a *wondrous difficulty* [*mirabilis dubitatio*], one must once more attempt [to determine] how unqualified coming to be occurs [*sit*], whether out of being in potency, or how it comes about in another way.

66 Aristotle, *De gen. et corr.* 1.3 (317a32-318a27); cf. Aquinas, *In De gen.* 1.6-7. In the *De generatione et corruptione* Aristotle ties the presentation of the nature of the primary matter to the question of how

perpetual generation is possible. On the supposition of a finite corporeal universe, the answer is that the generation of this is the corruption of that, and the corruption of this the generation of that. Thus, there appears the nature of matter as a subject of contraries, always subject to some form.

67 Aristotle, *Metaph.* 1.8 (988b28-29).

68 Cf. J. Owens, *History*, p. 6. Oddly, at p. 10, Fr. Owens sees Thales has having a place in the history of philosophy only because, as he sees it, Aristotle regarded Thales as providing "the beginning of natural philosophy." Aristotle surely includes Thales in a group of thinkers whose ambitions were decidedly *metaphysical*, speaking of "the causes of all things;" *Metaph.* 1.3 (983b1-21).

69 Aristotle, *Metaph.* 4.1 (1003a21-32); Aquinas, *CM* 4.1 (529-533). Socrates also, as presented by Plato in *Phaedo* 96A-B and 97B, 97E, saw the early physicists as seeking the causes of being.

70 Stephen Weinberg, *Dreams of a Final Theory* (New York: Pantheon, 1992), p. 58.

71 Of course, a true particle would not be merely a building block, but would have a nature of its own. I am speaking only of Weinberg's line of thinking. Cf. Wallace, "Are Elementary Particles Real?" mentioned above in n. 39.

72 Consider a debate between the present-day evolutionary philosopher Michael Ruse and different critics in the periodical *Research News and Opportunities in Science and Theology.* In vol. 2, no. 1, Sept. 2001, p. 26, Ruse presented himself as a "hard-line reductionist," speaking of "ontological reduction, where one tries to show that everything comes from

(or consists of) one or just a few basic substances."
He was then challenged by an evolutionary scientist,
Lothar Schäfer, in the vol. 2, n. 4, Dec. 2001 issue, p.
16. Schäfer accused Ruse of "halfway reductionism"
in his biology, presenting himself as seeing everything
emerging from "the order of quantum reality." Ruse
in reply distinguishes "between ontological reduction, the belief that all things are constituted from a
few (perhaps just one) basic substance(s); methodological reduction, the belief that the best scientific
strategy is to seek ever-smaller entities by which to
explain; and theoretical reduction, the belief that all
theories can be deduced from ever-more powerful
theories, ultimately just one theory of the physical
sciences." And he immediately continues: "At the
scientific level (not whether there is a religious, non-
natural dimension), I accept ontological reduction
and methodological reduction with enthusiasm. I
think there is one basic world stuff, and the way
to do good science is by seeking out ever-smaller
entities—genes good, molecules better." However, I
must note, concerning biology, that he continues: "I
have never accepted full-blown theoretical reduction;
even my earliest writings argue that evolutionary
biology is [*sic*] a teleological dimension that cannot
be eliminated."

73 Plato, *Sophist* 246C. The giants hold that "to be is to
be a body." Their adversaries locate being entirely in
certain intelligible and bodiless forms. The Platonic
spokesman, the Eleatic Stranger, affirms that we need
both: cf. 249C. Notice also that Aristotle, *Metaph.*
7.1 (1028b2-4), speaks of the question: "what being
is?" as "...always the subject of doubt...."

74 Cf. especially Aquinas, *De substantiis separatis* cc. 6-8.

75 Cf. *De substantiis separatis* c. 6, ll. 88-129.

76 Cf. Jean-Pierre Torrell, O.P., *Saint Thomas Aquinas: The Person and His Work*, trans. Robert Royal (Washington, D.C.: Catholic University of America Press, 1996), pp 300-303. Cf. also Étienne Gilson, *History of Christian Philosophy in the Middle Ages* (New York: Random House, 1955), pp. 416-420.

77 Cf. Johannes Capreolus, *Defensiones theologiae divi Thomae Aquinatis*, edd. C. Paban and T. Pègues (Turonibus: Alfred Cattier, 1900), vol. 4, p. 18 ff. (*In Sent.* 2.13.1). The first conclusion (pp. 18B-19A) is that God cannot bring it about that primary matter be without form. This is proved by texts from Thomas: *Quodlibet* 3.1.1; *ST* 1.66.1 (not quoted); *DP* 4.1; *Sent.* 2.12.1.4 (not quoted). Capreolus's article 2 contains objections to the conclusions, and to the first he has arguments from Duns Scotus and Gregory of Rimini. At the beginning of this presentation he says (p. 22A):

Indeed, many argue against the first (conclusion). However, I will present specially the arguments of Scotus and Gregory; for though many argued at the time against it, the *Corrector of the Corruptor* replied to them adequately.

On the would-be correctors of Thomas's doctrine and the correctors of them, cf. Gilson, *History*, pp. 411 and 730, nn. 57-58. The "corruptor" is William of La Mare, and his "correctors" are Richard Clapwell and Thomas of Sutton.

I consider this "many" significant. The inability to conceive of matter as completely bereft of actual being is part of what I mean by "perennial presocratism."

Capreolus presents two sets of arguments from Scotus, the first from the *Sent.* 2.12.2, and the second from his *Quaestiones super libros Metaphysicorum*, book 7.

78 Gilson, Étienne, *Elements of Christian Philosophy* (Garden City, N.Y.: Doubleday, 1960), p. 62.

79 Cf., for example, *ST* 1.115.1 *ad* 2:

...materia prima, quae est potentia pura, sicut Deus est actus purus.... [prime matter, which is pure potency, just as God is pure act....]

80 *ST* 1.54.1:...actualitas potentialitati repugnat.

Steven Baldner, in his very helpful paper, "Matter, Prime Matter, Elements," given at the Notre Dame University Maritain Center Thomistic Institute, 24 July, 1998 (available on the Maritain Center web page), mentions as present-day opponents of the doctrine of prime matter as pure potency Christopher Byrne, "Prime Matter and Actuality," *Journal of the History of Philosophy* 33.2 (1995) 197-224, and Robert Sokolowski, "Matter, Elements and Substance in Aristotle," *Journal of the History of Philosophy* 8 (1970) 263-288.

81 Thus Thomas sees intellectual immaturity in the presocratics; cf. *CM* 7.2 (1284):

The ancient philosophers, introducing this argument [that only matter is substance] were led astray by ignorance of substantial form. For they had not yet advanced far enough that their intellect lift itself to something that is above the objects of sense; and thus they considered only those forms which are the proper and the common objects of sense. Such [forms], however, are evidently accidents, such as the white and the black, the big and the small, and items of that order. Now, the substantial form is not an object of sense, save by association; and so they did not arrive at knowledge of it, so as to know how to distinguish it from matter. Rather, the entire subject, which we hold to be composed out of matter and form, they said was the primary matter, for example, air, or water, or something of that order. They called "forms" what we call "accidents," that is, such items as quantities and qualities, whose proper subject is not prime matter but rather the composite substance, which is substance in act. For, every accident *is* in virtue of this, that it *inheres* in substance, as has been said.

82 Aristotle does not define act, because it is a primary, simple (that is, non-complex) intelligibility and so does not admit of definition. A definition is meant to make known the defined item. Thus, the things one includes in the definition must themselves be *better known* than the thing one defines. Hence, the best known things of all cannot be defined, since nothing is better known than they are. In the line of analysis one must come eventually to things which are primary principles of intelligibility. "Being" and its divisions, "act," and "potency," are such principles. Accordingly, Aristotle begins his presentation of act or actuality by the statement, at *Metaph*. 9.6 (1048a30-32), trans. W. D. Ross:

Actuality [*energeia*], then, is the existence [*to huparchein*] of a thing not in the way which we express by "potentially."

83 Aquinas, *CM* 9.5 (1827).

84 Nevertheless, while form is "in" matter, it also "contains" matter. Thus we read at *ST* 1.8.1 *ad* 2:

> …though corporeal things are said to be "in" something as in what contains, nevertheless spiritual things *contain* those *in* which they are: as *the soul contains the body.*

Cf. Aristotle, *De anima* 1.5 (411b5-8), and Aquinas, *Sentencia libri De anima* 1.14, ll. 84-90. As regards substantial form generally, consider *ST* 1.29.2 *ad* 5: the substantial form is what gives subsistence to matter.

85 *ST* 1.8.1:

> Esse autem est illud quod est magis intimum cuilibet, et quod profundius omnibus inest, cum sit formale respectu omnium quae in re sunt, ut ex supra dictis patet. [Now, being is that which is most intimate to each thing and what is *most deeply within*, since it is *formal* with respect to all [items] that are in the thing, as is clear from things said earlier.]

The earlier texts meant are especially *ST* 1.4.1 *ad* 3 and *ST* 1.7.1. In the latter text we have:

> Illud autem quod est maxime formale omnium, est ipsum esse…. [That which is *most formal of all* is the very act of being….]

86 *ST* 2-2.8.1; the passage continues:

> Now, there are many sorts of thing which are "hidden inside" [as it were], regarding which it is necessary that human knowledge "penetrate to the interior," so to speak. Thus, "*within*" the accidents lies hidden the substantial nature of the thing; "*within*" words lie hidden the meanings of words; "*within*" likenesses and symbols lies hidden the symbolized truth; and effects *lie hidden*

in causes, and vice versa. Hence, with respect to all these cases, one can speak of "intellect."

Cf. also *ST* 2-2.180.5 *ad* 2:

…human contemplation, as found in the present life [as distinct from life after death], cannot be without images [in the imagination], because it is connatural to man that he see intelligible conceptions in images, as Aristotle says in *De anima* 3.7 (431a16). Nevertheless, intellectual knowledge does not come to rest in the images themselves, but in them it contemplates the purity of intelligible truth.

87　In this connection I recall the remarkable article by the Harvard zoologist, Steven Jay Gould, *New York Times*, February 19, 2001, entitled "Humbled by the Genome's Mysteries." Gould writes on the occasion of the discovery that the human genome possesses only "30,000 to 40,000 genes with the final tally almost sure to lie nearer the lower figure." It was previously known that the roundworm *C. elegans* contains only 959 cells and just over 19,000 genes. Accordingly, the general estimate of what the human being would require was well over 100,000, with 142,634 widely advertised as the "reasonable expectation." Gould says: "Human complexity cannot be generated by 30,000 genes under the old view of life." And: "Those 142,000 messages no doubt exist, as they must to build our bodies' complexity, with *our previous error now exposed as the assumption that each message came from a distinct gene*." And he explains: "From its late 17th century inception in modern form, science has strongly privileged the reductionist mode of thought that breaks overt complexity into constituent parts and then tries to explain the totality by the properties

of these parts and simple interactions fully predict-
able from the parts.... The collapse of the doctrine of
one gene for one protein, and one direction of causal
flow from basic codes to elaborate totality, marks the
failure of reductionism for the complex system that
we call biology" [italics added].

88 That the human soul subsists: Aquinas, *ST* 1.75.2;
    that it is pure form and not a composite of matter
    and form: *ST* 1.75.5.

89 Cf. *CM* 7.2 (1277).

90 *ST* 1.76.8 (461b5-26). Thomas goes on to say:

    A sign of this is that no part of a body has its proper
    operation, given the removal of the soul; whereas nev-
    ertheless everything which retains its species retains the
    operation of the species.

    Obviously, present-day transplant surgery raises a
    question here. The answer required by the nature of
    substance is that which we find in Aquinas, *In De
    gen.* 1.8 (60 [3]), concerning Aristotle, *De gen. et corr.*
    1.3 (318b1-14). There are incomplete or imperfect
    forms, as one moves from the living thing to its
    degenerate states.

91 *ST* 1.77.6 (ed. Ottawa, p. 469a25-40).

92 In a way this is clearer in the earlier treatment of
    this issue, at *Sent.* 1.8.5.3 *ad* 1 (ed. Mandonnet, p.
    234), where, in order to explain "totality" as regards
    form and essence, Thomas does not attempt to take
    "whole," generally, as "what is divided into parts, as
    he does in *ST* 1.76.8. Instead, he explains "totality"
    as said of form in its own distinctive way, as being
    the same as "perfect," meaning "that which is lacking
    in nothing (pertaining to it):"

...cum dicimus totam animam esse in qualibet parte corporis, intelligimus per totum perfectionem naturae suae, et non aliquam totalitatem partium; totum enim et perfectum est idem, ut dicit Philosophus. [...when we say that the whole soul is in every part whatsoever of the body, we understand by "whole" the complete perfection of its own nature and not some totality of parts: for "whole" and "perfect" are the same, as the Philosopher [Aristotle] says.]

Cf. Aristotle, *Phys.* 3.6 (207a8-15), and Aquinas, *CP* 3.11 (385 [4]). Cf. also Aristotle, *Metaph.* 5.16 (1021b12-23), and Aquinas, *CM* 5.18 (1033-1038); in this latter text, the perfection of form is fused with that of "magnitude of power," as in *ST* 1.42.1 *ad* 1.

93 See above, at n. 73.

94 Cf. Aristotle, *Metaph.* 7.3 (1029a33-34); Aquinas, *CM* 7.2 (1297-98). Cf. also Charles De Koninck, *The Hollow Universe* (London: Oxford University Press, 1960), ch. 3: "The Lifeless World of Biology" (and the entire book). While in the present essay I have focused on the error of the materialist side in the battle, Thomas, with Aristotle, also rejects the side represented by the Platonic doctrine of form and its corresponding epistemology: cf. Aquinas, *ST* 1.88.1 and 3 (and for the fundamental critique: *ST* 1.84.1).

95 Cf. above, n. 14.

96 Cf., for example, *CM* 4.2 (556 and 558) and *ST* 1.50.2 *ad* 3; also Thomas Aquinas, *Quaestiones disputatae de anima* 6, in *Opera omnia*, vol. 24.1; and *De substantiis separatis* 8.

97 In fact, such exemplar causality extends in diverse degrees to everything in the created thing, even the

primary matter: cf. *ST* 1.14.11 *ad* 3, and also above, n. 62; at *SCG* 1.70.3 Thomas even attributes a measure of nobility to potency through its order to act.

98 In so doing, one imitates Aristotle, as at *Metaph.* 8.2 (1042b14 ff.), using accidental differences analogous to the role of substantial form, as he explains at 1043a4-5. See also Aquinas, *CM* 8.2 (1696) and *CM* 7.2 (1277).

99 Aristotle, *Metaph.* 8.2 (1042b25-28) (italics in the Ross trans.).

100 Aquinas, *CM* 8.2 (1894):

Dicit ergo primo, quod quia praedictae differentiae sunt constitutivae rerum de quibus supra dictum est, manifestum quod ipsum esse praedictarum rerum toties dicitur quot sunt differentiae. Differentia enim complet definitionem significantem esse rei. Limen enim est huiusmodi, quia ita ponitur. Et ipsum sic poni est esse ipsius, idest propria eius ratio. Et similiter esse crystalli, est ipsum taliter inspissari.

101 *CM* 7.3 (1310):

But it must be known that in all the following, by the expression "being this" [*hoc esse*] or "being for this" [*huic esse*], he means the *quod quid erat esse* of that thing; for example, "being for man" [*homini esse*] or "being man" [*hominem esse*]: he means that which pertains to the "what is man."

At *Sent.* 1.33.1.1 *ad* 1 (ed. Mandonnet, pp. 765-766), three meanings of "*esse*" are given: the nature of the thing, the act of the essence (as "living" is the being of living things), and the truth of propositions. These meanings are given again in *Sent.* 3.6.2.2 (ed. Moos, n. 79, p. 238).

102 *ST* 1.14.6 (ed. Ottawa, p. 97b17-19):

> Et omnis forma, per quam quaelibet res in propria specie
> constituitur, perfectio quaedam est. [And every form,
> through which any thing whatsoever is established in its
> own species, is some perfection.]

103 *DP* 7.2 *ad* 9; and cf. *ST* 1.4.1 *ad* 3.

104 Cf. *DP* 7.2 obj. 10 and *ad* 10.

105 Cf. *SCG* 3.65.2400 and *ST* 1.104.1.

106 Cf. *ST* 1.104.1 (ed. Ottawa, pp. 622b-623a9).

107 Cf. Thomas Aquinas, *Questiones de quolibet* 12.4.1,
ll. 16-18, in *Opera omnia*, vol. 25:

> …unumquodque quod est in potentia et in actu, fit actu
> per hoc quod participat *actum superiorem*. […each thing
> which is in potency and in act is made to be in act inas-
> much as it participates *in a higher act*] [italics mine].

As the setting in the *quodlibet* makes clear, this
is true not only for the effect of change but also for
the effect of creative causality; cf. Thomas Aquinas,
Quaestiones disputatae de anima 6 *ad* 10, in *Opera
omnia*, vol. 24.1:

> …agens per motum reducit aliquid de potentia in actum;
> agens autem sine motu non reducit aliquid de potentia
> in actum, set facit esse actu id quod secundum naturam
> est in potentia ad esse. Et huiusmodi agens est creans.
> […that which acts through movement reduces some-
> thing from potency to act. But that which acts without
> movement does not reduce something from potency to
> act, but rather makes to be in act that which according
> to its own nature is in potency towards being. And what
> creates is an agent of this sort.

108 Accordingly, Thomas, arguing that God must be the first cause of form, uses the premise that God is the cause of being: *since being is caused by form and not by matter*, God must be first cause of form. Cf. *SCG* 2.43.8:

> Sicut esse est primum in effectibus, ita respondet primae causae ut proprius effectus. Esse autem est per formam, et non per materiam. Prima igitur causalitas formarum maxime est primae causae attribuenda. [Since being is first among effects, it corresponds to the first cause as its proper effect. But being is through form and not through matter. Therefore, the first causality of forms is to be attributed most of all to the first cause.]

109 Potency is for the sake of act, and thus the form is for the sake of the act of being. Cf. *DP* 7.2 *ad* 10 on the role of *esse* as *final* causal relative to the form or essence of the creature.

110 In the *Contra Gentiles* Thomas called this power-to-be "active" (*SCG* 1.20.174). Subsequently he denies this and calls it "receptive" (*CM* 12.8 [2550]: "*non...virtus activa sui esse, sed solum susceptiva;*" at *In De caelo* 1.6 (61 [5]), he says it is not passive (that is the potency of matter with respect to being) but rather "pertains to the potency of form." We are told in *ST* 1.104.4 *ad* 2:

> ...*potentia creaturae ad essendum est receptiva tantum*; sed potentia *activa* est ipsius *Dei*, a quo est influxus essendi. Unde quod res in infinitum durent, sequitur infinitatem divinae virtutis. Determinatur tamen quibusdam rebus virtus ad manendum tempore determinato, inquantum impediri possunt ne percipiant influxum essendi qui est ab eo, ex aliquo contrario agente, cui finita virtus non potest resistere tempore infinito, sed solum tempore

determinato. Et ideo ea quae non habent contrarium, *quamvis habeant finitam virtutem*, perseverant in aeternum. [...the potency of the creature towards being is receptive only; but the active power is that of God himself, from whom is the inflowing of being. Hence, that things endure forever follows upon the infinity of the divine power. However, there is determined for some things a power for enduring for determinate time, inasmuch as they can be impeded from receiving the influx of being which is from him, [impeded, that is] by some contrary agent, which [the determinate thing's] finite power cannot resist for an infinite time but only for a determinate time. Thus, things which have no contrary, though they have finite power, can endure forever.]

It seems to me that the most clarifying description of the potency of form, a description given in connection with the explanation of the perpetuity of perpetual things, is that found in *CP* 8.21 (1153 [13]). It is a potency towards *esse* and not at all a potency towards *non-esse*. Thomas criticizes Averroes there for thinking that all potency is towards opposites. The potency of form is simply towards *esse*.

111 *Sent.* 2.1.1.1 *ad* 5 (ed. Mandonnet, p. 16):

...forma, quae pars est rei, est similitudo agentis primi fluens ab ipso. Unde *omnes* formae reducuntur in primum agens sicut in principium exemplare....

112 *DP* 6.6 *ad* 5:

Ad quintum dicendum, quod secundum Philosophum, etiam in causis formalibus prius et posterius invenitur; unde nihil prohibet unam formam per alterius formae participationem formari; et sic ipse Deus, qui est esse tantum, est quodammodo species omnium formarum

subsistentium quae esse participant et non sunt suum
esse.

The context is the doctrine that angels, though
creatures, are pure forms subsisting, not matter-form
composites. The Latin term *"species"* is applied to
God because the objection cited Augustine calling
God the *"species"* that makes all things *"speciosa"* or
beautiful. This vocabulary for form reminds us of the
relation of form to beauty, which is itself character-
ized by light, *"claritas,"* in things. Thus, elsewhere
Thomas says, commenting on the pseudo-Dionysius,
in Thomas Aquinas, *In librum beati Dionysii De
divinis nominibus expositio*, ed. C. Pera (Rome-Turin:
Marietti, 1950), 4.5 (349):

> [Dionysius] says...that the being of all existents comes
> from this [divine] beauty: for clarity pertains to the
> consideration of beauty, as has been said. Now, every
> form, through which the thing has being, is some par-
> ticipation in the divine clarity. And this is what he adds,
> namely, that particular things are beautiful in function
> of their proper intelligible character, that is, in function
> of their proper form. Hence it is clear that the being of
> all is derived from the divine beauty.

113 *ST* 1.14.6:

> Propria enim natura uniuscuiusque consistit, secundum
> quod per aliquem modum divinam perfectionem partici-
> pat. Non autem Deus perfecte seipsum cognosceret, nisi
> cognosceret quomodocumque participabilis est ab aliis
> sua perfectio, nec etiam ipsam naturam essendi perfecte
> sciret, nisi cognosceret omnes modos essendi.

114 Cf. *ST* 1.42.1 *ad* 1 on quantity of power having
its root in form.

115 Thomas Aquinas, *Quaestiones disputatae de veritate*
     27.1 *ad* 3, ll. 182-186, in *Opera omnia*, vol. 22.3.

116 *DP* 5.1 *ad* 2.

117 *ST* 1.104 *ad* 1:

> ...esse per se consequitur formam creaturae, supposito
> tamen influxu Dei, sicut lumen sequitur diaphanum
> aeris, supposito influxu solis.

118 *ST* 2-2.23.2 *ad* 3:

> Ad tertium dicendum quod caritas operatur formaliter.
> *Efficacia autem formae est secundum virtutem agentis qui
> inducit formam.* Et ideo quod caritas non est vanitas, sed
> facit effectum infinitum dum coniungit animam Deo
> iustificando ipsam, hoc demonstrat infinitatem virtutis
> divinae, quae est caritatis auctor [italics mine].

The "vanity" of the creature is, of course, a recourse
by the objector to the language of, for example, *Psalm*
38.6, characterizing the creaturely substance, and
man in particular, as a mere shadow. Cf. Thomas
Aquinas, *In Psalmos Davidis expositio* 38.4, in
Aquinas, *Opera omnia ad fidem optimarum editio-
num acurate recognita* (Parma: Petrus Fiaccadorus,
1852-1873), vol. 14, where many Biblical parallels
are given.

119 *ST* 1.79.4 *ad* 5.

120 *ST* 1.7.1.

121 *ST* 1.4.1 *ad* 3; thus, in *ST* 1.8.1, the doctrine is
     repeated in arguing for God's presence in things:

> Esse autem est illud quod est magis intimum cuilibet,
> et quod profundius omnibus inest, cum sit formale
> respectu omnium quae in re sunt, ut ex supra dictis
> patet. [Being is that which is most intrinsic to any thing

whatsoever, and what is most deeply within, since it is formal with respect to all items that are in a thing, as was said earlier.]

122 Cf. *ST* 1-2.66.5 *ad* 4.

123 *ST* 1.19.6. Cf. the doctrine of the *Liber de causis*, prop. 1, in Thomas Aquinas, *Super Librum de causis expositio*, ed. H. D. Saffrey, O.P. (Fribourg-Louvain: Société philosophique-Nauwelaerts, 1954); Aquinas, *Commentary on the Book of Causes*, trans. Vincent A. Guagliardo, O.P., Charles R. Hess, O.P., and Richard C. Taylor (Washington, D.C.: Catholic University of America Press, 1996).

124 *DP* 3.5.

125 *ST* 1.4.2 (ed. Ottawa, p. 25a8-11).

126 Cf. *ST* 1.5.4 (ed. Ottawa, p. 30a35-38), where Thomas cites this teaching from Aristotle, *Meteorology* 4.3 (380a12).

127 *ST* 1.4.3.

128 Thus, St. Thomas envisaged an order, under God, of spiritual and corporeal natures, the angels and the celestial bodies, to account for the causing of substantial forms in the world of generation and corruption. Of course, the very first creation would require immediate divine origin of forms because their first presence in matter could not be a change from potency to act; cf. *ST* 1.65.4. The work of secondary causes is not envisaged by Thomas as in a context of evolution, that is, with the appearance of new species; however, he does not rule out such events, as is clear in *ST* 1.73.1 *ad* 3 (ed. Ottawa, p. 431b10-22), and the sort of active power considered in *ST* 1.110.2 *ad* 3 would allow the angels, working through the celestial bodies, such a role.

129 Cf. *ST* 1.116.1 (ed. Ottawa, pp. 691b38 -692a3):

> Quia nihil prohibet id quod est per accidens, accipi ut unum ab aliquo intellectu, alioquin intellectus formare non posset hanc propositionem, fodiens sepulcrum invenit thesaurum. Et sicut hoc potest intellectus apprehendere, ita potest efficere, sicut si aliquis sciens in quo loco sit thesaurus absconditus, instiget aliquem rusticum hoc ignorantem, ut ibi fodiat sepulcrum. Et sic nihil prohibet ea quae hic per accidens aguntur, ut fortuita vel casualia, reduci in aliquam causam ordinantem, quae per intellectum agat; et praecipue intellectum divinum. [Nothing prevents that which is by coincidence from being grasped as a unity by some intellect: otherwise one could not form the proposition: "the person digging the grave found the treasure." And just as the intellect can envisage this, so also it can make it happen; thus, for example, if someone knowing where a treasure is hidden prompts a workman unaware of this to dig a grave in that place. And thus nothing prevents those things which are effected here [in this world] by coincidence, such as lucky or chance occurrences, to be traced to some ordering cause which acts by intellect; and most especially to the divine intellect.]

130 On this cf. Armand Maurer, C.S.B., "Darwin, Thomists, and Secondary Causality," *Review of Metaphysics* 57 (2004) 491-514.

131 Cf. *SCG* 3.77 and 78.

132 Cf. *ST* 1.100.1 and 1.115.3.

133 Cf. Lawrence Dewan, "St. Thomas, the Fourth Way, and Creation," *Thomist* 59 (1995) 371-378, and "St. Thomas and Infinite Causal Regress," in

Idealism, Metaphysics, and Community, ed. W. Sweet (Aldershot, England: Ashgate, 2001), pp. 119-130.

134 Aristotle, *Metaph.* 12.6 (1071b22-31); cf. Thomas *CM* 12.6 (2501-2503).

THE AQUINAS LECTURES

Published by the Marquette University Press
Milwaukee WI 53201-1881 USA
All volumes available as ebooks. See web page:
http://www.marquette.edu/mupress/

14. *St. Thomas and the World State.* Robert M. Hutchins (1949) ISBN 0-87462-114-3

15. *Method in Metaphysics.* Robert J. Henle, S.J. (1950) ISBN 0-87462-115-1

16. *Wisdom and Love in St. Thomas Aquinas.* Étienne Gilson (1951) ISBN 0-87462-116-X

17. *The Good in Existential Metaphysics.* Elizabeth G. Salmon (1952) ISBN 0-87462-117-8

18. *St. Thomas and the Object of Geometry.* Vincent E. Smith (1953) ISBN 0-87462-118-6

19. *Realism And Nominalism Revisted.* Henry Veatch (1954) ISBN 0-87462-119-4

20. *Imprudence in St. Thomas Aquinas.* Charles J. O'Neil (1955) ISBN 0-87462-120-8

21. *The Truth That Frees.* Gerard Smith, S.J. (1956) ISBN 0-87462-121-6

22. *St. Thomas and the Future of Metaphysics.* Joseph Owens, C.Ss.R. (1957) ISBN 0-87462-122-4

23. *Thomas and the Physics of 1958: A Confrontation.* Henry Margenau (1958) ISBN 0-87462-123-2

24. *Metaphysics and Ideology.* Wm. Oliver Martin (1959) ISBN 0-87462-124-0

25. *Language, Truth and Poetry.* Victor M. Hamm (1960) ISBN 0-87462-125-9

26. *Metaphysics and Historicity.* Emil L. Fackenheim (1961) ISBN 0-87462-126-7

27. *The Lure of Wisdom.* James D. Collins (1962) ISBN 0-87462-127-5

28. *Religion and Art.* Paul Weiss (1963) ISBN 0-87462-128-3

29. *St. Thomas and Philosophy.* Anton C. Pegis (1964) ISBN 0-87462-129-1

30. *The University in Process.* John O. Riedl (1965) ISBN 0-87462-130-5

31. *The Pragmatic Meaning of God.* Robert O. Johann (1966) ISBN 0-87462-131-3

32. *Religion and Empiricism.* John E. Smith (1967) ISBN 0-87462-132-1

33. *The Subject.* Bernard Lonergan, S.J. (1968) ISBN 0-87462-133-X

34. *Beyond Trinity.* Bernard J. Cooke (1969) ISBN 0-87462-134-8

35. *Ideas and Concepts.* Julius R. Weinberg (1970) ISBN 0-87462-135-6

36. *Reason and Faith Revisited.* Francis H. Parker (1971) ISBN 0-87462-136-4

37. *Psyche and Cerebrum.* John N. Findlay (1972) ISBN 0-87462-137-2

38. *The Problem of the Criterion.* Roderick M. Chisholm (1973) ISBN 0-87462-138-0

39. *Man as Infinite Spirit.* James H. Robb (1974) ISBN 0-87462-139-9

40. *Aquinas to Whitehead: Seven Centuries of Metaphysics of Religion.* Charles Hartshorne (1976) ISBN 0-87462-141-0

41. *The Problem of Evil.* Errol E. Harris (1977) ISBN 0-87462-142-9

42. *The Catholic University and the Faith.* Francis C. Wade, S.J. (1978) ISBN 0-87462-143-7

43. *St. Thomas and Historicity.* Armand J. Maurer, C.S.B. (1979) ISBN 0-87462-144-5

44. *Does God Have a Nature?* Alvin Plantinga (1980) ISBN 0-87462-145-3

45. *Rhyme and Reason: St. Thomas and Modes of Discourse.* Ralph Mcinerny (1981) ISBN 0-87462-148-8

46. *The Gift: Creation.* Kenneth L. Schmitz (1982) ISBN 0-87462-149-6

62. *Science, Religion and Authority: Lessons from the Galileo Affair.* Richard J. Blackwell. (1998) ISBN 0-87462-165-8

63. *What Sort of Human Nature? Medieval Philosophy and the Systematics of Christology.* Marilyn McCord Adams. (1999) ISBN 0-87462-166-6

64. *On Inoculating Moral Philosophy against God.* John M. Rist. (2000) ISBN 0-87462-167-X.

65. *A Sensible Metaphysical Realism.* William P. Alston (2001) ISBN 0-87462-168-2.

66. *Eschatological Themes in Medieval Jewish Philosophy.* Arthur Hyman. (2002) ISBN 0-87462-169-0

67. *Old Wine in New Skins.* Jorge J. E. Gracia. (2003) ISBN 0-87462-170-4.

68. *The Metamorphoses of Phenomenological Reduction.* Jacques Tamininaux. (2004) ISBN 0-87462-171-2.

69. *Common Sense: A New Look at an Old Philosophical Tradition.* (2005) ISBN-10: 0-87462-172-0; ISBN-13:978-0-87462-172-3.

70. *Five Metaphysical Paradoxes.* Howard P. Kainz. (2006) ISBN: 0-87462-173-9; ISBN-13: 978-0-87462-173-0.

71. *St. Thomas and Form as Something Divine in Things.* Lawrence Dewan, O.P. (2007) ISBN 978-0-87462-174-7.